Exorcism At Midnight

Leander Jackie Grogan

groganbooks.com

Publishing Services Worldwide

Third Edition

For information on permissions, email:
permissions@groganbooks.com.

Visit website at: www.groganbooks.com

Printed in the United States of America
Third Printing: June, 2016
ISBN-978-1-62407-119-5

BOOKS BY LEANDER JACKIE GROGAN

Orange FingerTips

Exorcism At Midnight

The Blood Tears Of Jesus

Baby, Put That Gun Down

Layoff Skullduggery: The Official Humor Guide

King Juba's Chest

Black Church Blues

The Bible Gobbled Up My Big Sister [Not yet released]

What's Wrong With Your Small Business Team? [Nonfiction Bestseller]

About the Author

Leander Jackie Grogan's excellence in writing extends over a multiplicity of genres. His eight novels have been distributed in eleven countries and five different languages. He has won numerous local and national awards in creative writing for radio, print and the web. Besides having authored a number of nonfiction articles in such national magazines as AdWeek and Jet, and a business bestseller, What's Wrong With Your Small Business Team?, Grogan serves as a guest blogger for the national crime/suspense writer's website, Murder by 4, has written and produced three local spiritual comedies, and some years ago, had a work of fiction published in Hustler Magazine.

Grogan's popularity continues to grow exponentially as a member of the new breed of storytellers unencumbered by the dictates of old world cookie-cutter characters and a narrow spotlight, perpetually shining on the rich side of town. His characters are bold and edgy and unpredictable, and invariably in conflict with traditional values. His writing explores spiritual unknowns and the deep crevices of the mind that harbor raw insights and indelible truths.

"Do not follow where the path may lead. Go, instead, where there is no path and leave a trail."
-Ralph Waldo Emerson-

Dedication

This book is dedicated to the unknown seekers of truth who, at the gateway of knowledge, have been turned away by religious traditionalists that oppose any form of learning beyond the status quo. The world is not flat. Columbus did not discover America. And, demon possession is real.

A spiritual interlude in time when Protestants and Catholics bind inseparably to fight pure evil...

INTRODUCTION

The story you are about to read is mind-boggling, high-intensity fiction. However, the phenomenon it describes is centered in bone-chilling reality.

Demonic possession is loosely defined as the control of an individual by supernatural beings such as Satan and/or his demons and imps. Symptoms accompanying demonic possession may include erased or altered memories and personalities, discernible changes in vocal intonation and facial structure, episodes of convulsions and fits, abilities to speak in foreign languages, and unexplained knowledge (gnosis) about the past or future.

Though, the Bible offers many accounts of demon possession, some modern-day evangelical Christians and other official church denominations avoid the subject and discourage its teaching or exploration. In essence, they have unofficially extracted or voided portions of the Scripture.

I believe in the great truths of the Bible. That is my definitive source for understanding what happens in the invisible or supernatural world. The Bible says that demons got into or possessed people in ancient times. So I believe that. Just because we disapprove of an action, we cannot afford to avoid it, altogether. I disapprove of slavery. So should I deny it ever existed or refuse to discuss it?

At the same time, we must be careful not to glamorize the power of evil or take a lackluster approach to its diabolical objective and design. Those individuals seeking knowledge through *Ouija* (weegie) boards, tarot cards, black cat bone, hexes and spells are involved in devil worship, which opens them up to possession. They are asking a source of superior power in the supernatural world to share that power with them in order to give them an edge in the natural world. This requires submission and obedience to that source. This blatant invitation is how many people find themselves tormented by evil spirits.

On February 19, 2002, the late Pope John Paul reported that he had been involved in three Exorcisms during his tenure as a Roman Catholic Priest. Inside sources indicated that Pope John Paul felt the official office of exorcists needed to be given more attention and restored to the priesthood. His reasoning was simple. The cases of demon possession in contemporary societies all over the world were exploding. From his perspective, this unspeakable spiritual crisis could no longer be ignored.

Finally, if there is an alternative thread to this incredible journey, it's the examination of suffering in our lives. We all suffer. At some point, we all ask why. *Exorcism At Midnight* provides spiritual insight into the phases of suffering and the invisible catalysts that usher suffering into our lives.

Now, on to the journey. Examine. Explore. Enjoy!

Chapter One

*A*t bedtime, I took one last look out of my window. Dark clouds slithered across the Houston skyline like billowed ghosts on parade. The cluster of needle pines in the front yard swayed back and forth like helpless dancers in an operetta of doom. An angry breeze whistled through my tattered window screen, perhaps an ominous prediction of things to come.

Two hundred miles away, a monster hurricane lingered off the Galveston coastline in the Gulf of Mexico, waiting for a signal from heaven or hell. To me, however, the storm's impending landfall was small potatoes compared to the journey that lay ahead.

The call had come in. The decision had been made. The fate of four demented souls had been locked into a precarious eternity. We were going forward with the exorcism at midnight. No further discussion -- not even the one that cried out from our subconscious minds, warning us about plunging into a dark, uncharted, metaphysical world -- was required.

Standing in front of the bathroom mirror, I gazed disappointedly at the black, bearded face, pushing out from my chunky neck and blubbered chest. It was a sad face with withered, eggshell eyes; the kind of face providence usually pasted behind the flowing tears of a condemned prisoner, headed for a firing squad. It was an appropriate face that complemented my slumping shoulders, budging gut and battle-weary knees. At thirty-eight, my body had severed all ties with the powerful fullback physic that had propelled our high school team to the state championship game back in '76. Rodney Coleman, *The Bull,* was the name with which the sports writers had bestowed upon me with such unanimous adoration. But now the merciless glass reflected a different image, a pitiful image, a shameful freeze-frame of Rodney Coleman, the flabby old buffalo, tormented by inflated memories of fame and what could've been.

Maybe, if I had managed to stay out of trouble at Texas A&M my junior year. Maybe, if I had avoided the fun-loving, ever seductive cocaine crowd. My coach had referred to me as his first football intellectual, a welcomed combination of brains and brawn. But sometimes confidence can be a great deceiver. Youthful invincibility has a way of leading you down the murky alleyways of life where the warning signs are shrouded in darkness.

Ironically, cocaine had been the improbable agent that guided me back to the light.

One night at an off-campus freebasing party, bad drugs from a Mexican cartel dealer had killed everyone but me ... well, me and a beautiful young honey brown, hazel eyed freshman whose prudish values and high-minded upbringing made her believe she had the right to be there with the superstar movers and shakers and not feel the slightest obligation to indulge. She became the only unscaved bystander, watching in horror as the plush condominium that college boosters had provided for our elite pleasures slowly transformed into a grisly death trap. By the time the ambulances stopped rolling and the paramedics finished their gruesome work, four star athletes and three sorority beauty queens lay dead in the city morgue.

The way my heart pounded with each frightful, precarious beat; the way my eyeballs bulged, sealing in the ominous lights that raced through my head; I, too, should've died. But interspersed between the red, yellow and green lights was a white light emanating from an awesome spirit-like figure in a faraway place, a peaceful, surreal place where the air was heavy with sweet ginger and the trees glistened like crystal. He showed me a giant bronze trunk with golden locks. Huge winged creatures with crimson eyes surrounded the trunk on all sides, as if protecting its contents from some invisible foe.

"Inside this trunk," he said, "are the mistakes of your past. You have a second chance."

Who was I to get a second chance? Of the athletes, groupies and hangers-on that made up our fun-loving crew, I was the least deserving. I was brash and cocky, an athlete's athlete, craving the limelight and used to getting my way. If there was a place at the back of the line for disqualified applicants, unworthy of reprieve, I owned it, lock, stock and barrel.

Yet, I heard the words. They were like thunderous rapids, flowing down the mountainside in early spring, washing the soot and pollution from the deep crevices of my mind. *"You have a second chance."*

After that bizarre night of death, and for me, resurrection, everything changed. Whether driven by fear, love, obedience or

13

a sense of obligation, I enrolled in a hometown seminary and became a minister. Kathy, the beautiful young freshman who had refused the lure of our tragic booze and drug fest, followed me back to Dallas to become my wife.

It was during these early years that I first met an immigrant named Yacine Bouteflilau. I could never pronounce his last name. So I stopped trying. Yet, from the very moment I met him, he stirred my fascination.

Yacine represented the epitome of miscegenation, the growing fusion of cultures from around the globe. His mother was from Algeria; his father, from Jordan. He had lived half his twenty-nine years in the African country of Angola before disease killed his parents. A Kansas missionary sponsored his immigration to America where a religious Scientology foundation underwrote his admission to seminary.

Dallas Theological Seminary was a quiet, secluded campus of tall green trees, luscious purple and blue flower gardens and stately tan brick buildings that sprawled over several acres of prime real estate in Dallas' west suburbs. Some evenings just before dusk, the wind, whistling through the exalted exterior archways, sounded like voices from heaven. No one dispelled the idea. It seemed only fitting that if God was going to speak, he'd do it where the vast inventories of scholarly Bibles outnumbered all of the other great spiritual repositories around the city. Southern Methodist University and Texas Christian University had become too commercial, too focused on winning the BCS and Final Four. There was no need to waste a heavenly lecture on lukewarm backsliders when Dallas Theological Seminary, the zealots of the Bible belt, were right across town, longing to absorb every glorious word from on high.

Dallas Theological Seminary had a proud history of turning out quality leaders who went on to make their mark in the Kingdom. That's why we were there ... to learn how to please God and make our mark. That was the scarlet robe of expectation that cloaked our young, eager, naive souls. That was the driving ambition that made us step forth as God's hand-picked liberators of a world darkened by sin. We were there to usher in good and keep humanity from going to hell in a hand basket. None of us had a clue how costly such a noble undertaking could be.

One night, after an eschatology class in the main auditorium, Yacine approached me. Thin-faced, with bushy black hair and piercing gray eyes, he reminded me of a young Mouammar Kadhafi.

"Maybe I talk to you?" He asked in a condescending voice. He was obviously still struggling with the language.

"This is not a good time," I had explained, never once breaking my accelerated stride. "I've got somewhere important I need to be."

I wondered why this foreigner had singled me out from a class of thirty. And yet, I didn't want to come off as being rude. I was trying to get to a late-night meeting at the Exall Recreation Center downtown. An informal search committee had been looking for someone to pastor a small church in Oakdale. Dr. Grossman, my assistant dean and personal mentor, had thrown my name into the hat.

"You're a perfect fit," he had told me in the prep session. "You're a hometown boy that knows the area, and you're not afraid to get your hands dirty with issues unique to the inner city."

It was his way of telling me the liquor stores and peep shows that surrounded the church on every block would be a challenge, but nothing a former project dweller and latchkey kid couldn't overcome.

Thanks to the love of my dear grandmother, I had overcome a missing-in-action mother on drugs and an absentee father who took pride in dropping nameless babies on every street corner. If he didn't learn their names, he didn't have to pay child support. That was his ingenious philosophy. That's what kept him slipping away in the night.

Thanks to the perseverance of my eleventh grade English teacher, Mr. Bryant, I had overcome saggin' pants, fake gold necklaces and ghetto slang. I had already tasted the bitter crumbs of life. What chance did a few liquor stores and peep shows have against an overcomer like me?

I was thrilled at the possibility. There was no better place to get hands-on training than a small church on the rough side of town where every problem was serious and every opportunity to help, a meaningful contribution. I would know all of my members by name. And I would lead them, boldly, out of the darkness and into the marvelous light. AND ... I would get paid for doing it; a much needed addition to my student loan refund check and part-time wages from working at the campus bookstore.

It seemed like a God-sent opportunity. I wasn't going to let a dopey-eyed foreigner with a bad accent get in the way.

When I arrived at the Center, the decision had already been made. Somebody's brother's nephew's cousin's godson with connections to the Board had finagled the position during a closed-door, smoky room vote.

It shouldn't have surprised me. Historically, these pastoral selection procedures were more political than spiritual. Nevertheless, having wasted my time and a third of a tank of

$4.00 a gallon gasoline, I was pissed. Even more alarming was the site of Yacine, standing outside of the Center, in the front parking lot.

"You followed me here? Who gave you that right?" I scolded him in a loud voice.

"You will talk to me now?" he persisted.

"NO! Matter of fact, you best stay out of my face." I flexed a few fullback muscles just to let him know I meant business.

The next night after class, he handed me an envelope, then walked away. Opening it, I discovered a full-color, detailed drawing of the bronze trunk with the golden locks, the precise trunk I had seen during my drug overdose.

A few days later, when classes resumed, I sought him out. "You've got my attention. Now tell me what this is all about."

His tone was just above a whisper. "You have the mark, the mark of suffering. You will serve God in a special way." Yacine went on to explain that through his multiple studies of Christianity, Judaism, Hinduism and Islam, he had come to believe that each living soul had a mark; an invisible, spiritual mark that specified their true calling.

I had read similar writings by Jung and other philosophers. The Bible even referred to a mark or seal placed on believers that members of the spirit world recognized.

"How does this mark look?" I inquired.

"You do not see it as such. You feel it." He pointed to a tall, balding man with a chiseled face, dressed in a black suit. He stood by the podium, speaking quietly to our distinguished, gray haired class instructor, Dr. Roosevelt Bingham. Throughout their exchange, the man brandished a perpetually disarming smile.

"This man has the mark of betrayal. You can feel it, yes?"

"No," I admitted.

"Don't worry, you will."

A few days later we learned Dr. Bingham, one of the most popular professors at the school, had been fired. Uncomfortable with the professor's growing influence over the students, the ball headed man had orchestrated a convoluted witch-hunt behind closed doors, something about the professor selfishly promoting himself over the school and the Word of God.

Dr. Bingham was a good man, a capable, caring instructor. And yet, he was unceremoniously removed, gone in a flash. That was my hash introduction to God's permissive will.

Over the remaining five months, Yacine and I became the closest of friends. Though he was only a few years older than me, I learned more from him than I had in all my years at seminary. It was not to say the school's curriculum was inadequate. It just appeared Yacine was so advanced in his understanding of the entire spiritual scheme of things.

In one class, Yacine unintentionally embarrassed a new instructor by asking him a heavy weight question about the true location of Mount Sinai, the holy mountain to which Moses had brought the children of Israel. Not wanting to admit he didn't know, the instructor rambled on for a while before scolding Yacine for taking the class off course. In another class, Yacine created an unsolvable dilemma for the professor by proving, Biblically, that prayer would not help the world get better because scripture had already declared that, as we moved toward the end times, it would get worse, and no prayer would make the Bible turn on its own prophecies.

I was always amused at how hard the instructors worked to suppress his input. Sometimes, he would be called into the office and reprimanded. Other times, the professors would simply disqualify his questions as being outside the scope of study and detrimental to the progress of the class. The more I tried to soak in his wisdom, the more the instructors tried to ring it out of existence. I found the equilibrium to be quite favorable because the less they allowed him to share in class, the more he shared with me.

"The suppression of knowledge among evangelical believers is no different from the tyrants and dictators in my part of the world," he declared. "They hold on to power by keeping the people from knowing the truth."

A week before graduation, my official mentor, Assistant Dean Grossman, a short, jolly man with silver-rimmed glasses and a rounded face, stopped me in the hallway. "I see you with Yacine quite often. How well do you know him?"

"We're friends. Why do you ask?"

He surveyed the area to make sure no one was around. "I'm telling you this in the strictest of confidence."

I nodded with acknowledgement.

"The young man prophesied in my life," he announced.

I tried to keep a straight face. I was thinking, *what's the big deal?* This is seminary. People walk around all the time prophesying, claiming to see visions and angels and hearing God's voice. Just a few weeks earlier, one of our classmates had to be rushed to the hospital for going on a hunger strike until, in his words, "Peace came to Jerusalem."

With a perplexed look on his face, he revealed, "Everything came true, just as he said."

Six months earlier, Yacine had told Dr. Grossman he would

come into a financial windfall, a *season of inheritance,* he had called it. He had warned Dr. Grossman to give it all away.

Dr. Grossman recalled, "Our parents left us fifteen acres of farmland down in Louisiana. A wildcatter contacted us, wanting to drill on the property. My brother and I agreed. We just signed the papers and forgot about it. Next thing I knew, they'd struck oil. They offered us a sweet buyout deal. We ended up splitting $425,000."

"Did you give your portion away?" I asked with a hint of sarcasm.

"Excuse my French, but hell no!" he replied. "I'm sixty-one years old. I've never seen that kind of money in my whole life."

"Any regrets, I mean, about keeping it against Yacine's advice?"

"Plenty," he admitted. "My wife asked if she could get her chin fixed, which turned out to be her chin, nose and you know..." He cupped both hands in front of his chest.

"So now she's three times as beautiful?" I speculated out loud.

He shook his head. "I wouldn't know. She ran off with our dentist. Turned out he was polishing a lot more than her teeth."

Dr. Grossman went on to explain that he was being sued by a contractor who remodeled their house, audited by the IRS, hounded by the State of Louisiana for inheritance taxes, and given the runaround by the dealership that sold him a brand new Lincoln lemon.

"My Corvette is wonderful," he boasted. "But this Lincoln is giving me the blues."

"I hope you don't blame Yacine for all of this?" I asked.

"On the contrary. The young man is a true ... something or other. I wanted to thank him for at least trying to warn me. But he, well, won't talk to me now."

I frowned. "What do you mean?"

"Last time I saw him, he just handed me this sketch." Dr. Grossman reached inside his coat pocket to reveal a drawing of a steel blue, closed casket. "Any idea what this means?"

It was two months after graduation that we learned the answer. Dr. Grossman got rid of the Lincoln and kept the Corvette. It was a young man's car that made him feel young again; so young that one night he wrapped it around an oak tree at 110 mph. His body was so badly burned that, at the funeral services, they were unable to open his casket ... his steel blue casket.

I never told Yacine about my encounter with Dr. Grossman. But somehow, I felt he knew. As we grew closer, there were things we shared on a cosmic level, never spoken and yet clearly understood. He also related well to Kathy. She often baked him raisin cookies and some kind of sweet Algerian *Warka*, a recipe she had found in an old Mediterranean cookbook.

It didn't surprise me when Yacine told her the *Warka* tasted exactly like the ones his mother used to make. With Kathy's homegrown Louisiana culinary skills and natural desire to accommodate others, the exquisite taste of the pastries and love she put into every dish she baked was merely an extension of her nurturing personality.

Yacine became a constant visitor to our cramped Southside apartment, always bearing some new Mediterranean trinket or cooking utensil or recipe for Kathy. He brought Biblical reference book and antique maps of the Holy Land for me. His intriguing stories of life in Africa and the Mideast mesmerized our inquiring spirits and opened us up to cultures we had never known. Indeed, he was a true ... something or other. One day I would find out what.

Chapter Two

"*But there is suffering in life, and there are defeats. No one can avoid them. But it's better to lose some of the battles in the struggles for your dreams than to be defeated without ever knowing what you're fighting for...*"

Paulo Coelho

*U*pon graduation, we vowed to stay in touch. Kathy and I moved to Houston to pastor a small Methodist church on the north side of town in the underprivileged Kashmere Gardens area. Yacine moved to upper New York State to study at the Saint Bonaventure Shrine under the legendary Franciscan priest, Frank Devann. Still, not a week went by without a phone call or text or email on our overpriced smartphones and tablets.

There was something about true friendship that disintegrated the miles between us. It was as though New York was right around the corner, and for him, Houston, a subway ride away.

Whenever Yacine left the country, he sent us postcards and often called to describe his African missionary work, sharing his growing dilemma between marrying one of the pretty girls he met during his stopovers in London or becoming a full-fledged priest.

"There is a timeless beauty in the word of God, as in nothing else." He would always come back to his deeply embedded spiritual roots. Both, Kathy and I were betting on his ultimate matrimony to the priesthood.

On our fifth wedding anniversary, Yacine flew down from New York to help us celebrate. He brought an 18 carat gold-plated cross he had purchased on a trip to Jerusalem. We were thrilled to hang it over our marble fireplace. It was a fitting addition to our yuppie Christian lifestyle.

At the time, Kathy had just turned twenty-five. Still bright, bubbly and glowing with a zeal for the ministry, she was pregnant with our first child. My name was at the very top of the list to pastor the Foundry United Methodist congregation, fifth largest church in the local United Methodist system. We had bought a new four bedroom, two story contemporary brick home in suburban Lexington Estates. Remarkably, in just three years, Kathy's catering business had doubled in volume, with a huge contract pending at the airport. There was no question in our minds. God was good ... good all the time.

That was when Yacine told me, "Your season has begun."

"*Season?*" I didn't understand what he meant.

"The stars have aligned," he said. "There is nothing that can be done."

These were his last words before returning to New York.

As a devoted evangelical minister, I didn't pay much

attention to the alignment of the stars. It was too close to astrology, too akin to the pagan Babylon worship that attempted to supplant the Creator of the Universe with little man-made gods and goddesses; those seductive polytheistic imposers, fashioned from wood and stone. Why should I care about the stars and their alignment? God was the one who made them. He kept them from crashing to earth and falling into the sea.

"Give God the glory, if for nothing else, keeping his magnificent universe from caving in on us," I often told my little 200-member congregation. *"There is no need to worry. God is in control."*

The following week, a weird blue orb of lightning struck our little northside church and burned it to the ground. No one could explain it. No one had ever seen blue lightning before nor witnessed mother nature's blistering assault on God's holy sanctuary. After a financially charged, closed-door meeting, with little in the way of a plausible explanation, the Elders decided not to rebuild.

The very next day, the selection committee from downtown informed me the number two candidate on their list had been chosen to pastor the Foundry Church. Although I had more qualifications, he was - according to them - a better fit.

What did they mean, *a better fit?* Of course, I didn't agree and requested a face-to-face meeting to further explore the matter. Like the smoky room deal at the Exall Recreation Center in Dallas, the whole thing had a bad smell.

The next week, on my way to the meeting, I received a call from my older sister, Patrice. She was a divorced mother of three, struggling to raise a troubled teenage daughter while holding down two jobs. She had been instrumental in convincing us to come to Houston, partly because of the opportunities that awaited us and partly because she hoped the involvement of a Godly uncle would help to turn her daughter's life around.

"Preacher." That's what everyone called me after seminary. Knowing the intimate details of my miraculous turnabout from the wild parties and weekend drug binges, she was exceedingly proud to call me by my new name.

There's a verse in the Bible that says a prophet is not welcome in his own home town. It's another way of saying people who knew you before you became a preacher are more inclined to hold on to the former images of your reeking havoc in the lives of everyone around you and wallowing in the mud. They don't trust your newly proclaimed holiness until it can be tested in a crisis. Patrice had been no exception to the wait-and-see rule.

One night, a year or so after we had moved to Houston, Patrice had called, hysterical and panic-stricken. Her drunken ex-husband had parked in the driveway, started honking his horn and demanding she come outside. By the time I arrived, he had kicked in the door and threatened the whole family with a .45 automatic.

In my old days, I would've taken away the pistol and squashed him like a bug. Instead, I walked right past him and the pistol, sat down on the sofa and started reading aloud from my Bible. The scriptures about God entrusting man to love, protect and be the head of his family from the very beginning of creation finally brought him to tears. She later told me that was the moment in time she knew I had changed. From that day forward, she called me preacher, too.

"Preacher," she said. "We're at Memorial Herman Hospital in the Medical Center. Kathy is fine, but ... she lost the baby."

The ominous news rushed out of my cell phone like a blazing fire, scorched my eardrums and sent me into mild convulsions. It took a while to realize, in that instant of shock and desperation, I had rear-ended a Latino family's green van. Some of the passengers jumped out and ran away. The two men who remained at the scene, however, spoke, briefly, to police, then headed to the nearest law office to sue.

I drove like a mad man through the heavy traffic to the Medical Center downtown. The parking garage was full. The main elevator was broken. Quickly navigating several flights of stairs, I finally entered Kathy's sterile, dark room. My sister was sitting in a corner chair, crying her eyes out. Kathy laid in bed like a zombie, motionless to the point of death. Heavily sedated with bloodshot eyes, she managed one disconcerting question: "Why did God take our child?"

After that, she drifted off into a hopeless oblivion.

During my wild and foolish exploits at Texas A&M, a cocaine overdose had summoned the Angel of Death to my doorstep. During those perilous hours when blazing colors and resounding voices filled my head, God had taken me to a place of untold radiance and beauty and showed me a mystery. From a distant mountain valley of fertile green foliage streamed a bright red river of blood. It was a deep river with swirling currents that carried the souls of unborn babies to their earthly dimension.

But to my awakening sorry, some never made it. Trolling beneath the currents were deadly soul eaters ... bloated, stealthy, rat-faced creatures with dark eyes and jagged teeth that rose up from the abyss to swallow a single defenseless translucent embryo with one methodical crunch.

Like Paul visiting the Third Heaven, I never deciphered the full meaning of the vision, just that God was fully aware of the creatures and the specific souls that would never come into the earth's realm. From that moment on, my heart ached with unspeakable compassion each time I heard the news of an abortion or miscarriage or still born. Now, my child was among the young souls that never made it through.

It took about ten months for us to lose our home, our catering business and our good standing in the community. Our lives gradually transformed into a surreal nightmare, foggy, dismal and filled with new iterations of pain and distress. It was as though we were sleepwalking on hot coals with invisible ice picks, stabbing us in the back.

Someone speculated out loud the church Elders in Kashmere Gardens had found financial discrepancies. That's why they had opted not to rebuild our little church. Of course, that was a lie. But in a world of cell phones, emails, Twitter and Facebook, a juicy lie could take flight more easily than the boring truth.

No church wanted me as their pastor. In fact, while visiting one church in the Third Ward area, the pastor inadvertently announced to his congregation that they should not be so eager criticize. Rather, they should pray for me and Kathy because "no one was perfect."

"Did you hear him?!!" Kathy fumed all the way home. "He said no one was perfect, as if we had done something wrong, as if we had brought this on ourselves." And then she began to cry.

I didn't answer. I had no answer. In all of the many Bibles and Books of Commentary and religious documentaries I owned, I couldn't find an example where God had taken his own lightning and burned down his own church. He had burned down Sodom & Gomorrah. He had burned up the disobedient Israelites who worshiped the golden calf. But God didn't hurt his own people. He took care of his own ... didn't he?

Kathy took a job in a Kroger's bakery department while I ran rural routes for the Post Office, part-time. We managed to find a small, two-story, two-bedroom, wood frame rental house in the ship channel district. In a desperate attempt to fortify our own faith, we started hosting a Bible study for a few couples in the neighborhood.

It was two years into our meager existence, living from check-to-check. That's when our marriage began to crumble.

One Friday night, after all of the Bible study members had gone home, I finished stacking the folding chairs in the garage. Finding a cushy spot on the living room sofa, I sipped on a cup of reheated coffee and tried to calm my nerves. It was hard work teaching the goodness of God while suffering under his enormous wrath. I had to go into myself, then come out of myself, then forget about myself in order to concentrate on my obligation to the Kingdom and its people. We were holy vessels, channels for righteousness, instruments of light. At least, that's what they had told us at seminary. But how difficult it was for the light to find its way through the darkened, feeble, beaten down channels we had become.

Kathy sat in the big blue flowered armchair across from me, staring with hardened eyes. "Why are we doing this? Why are we still serving a God that has turned his back on us?"

"We're in a season," I reassured her. "Sooner or later we'll come out. And we'll be just fine."

"Are you sure, Rodney?" she asked, pleading for her man

of God to declare an end to the misery. "Do you promise me this won't go on forever?"

I tried to hide my anxiety. The question she posed, however, was profound and unsettling. It took me back to an unforgettable day at seminary when Yacine had pressed another professor against the wall. This was not just any professor, but Dr. Jeremiah McCormack, an old white haired, ultra-conservative instructor, dean and member of the Board. He was a very powerful man in his own right. With one phone call, he could raise half a million dollars for the school's latest expansion project. He was notorious for locking his classroom door one minute after the designated start time. And if you made an eighty-nine on your test, then that was your grade. If you wanted the extra point, then you should've studied harder.

If you were going to go up against someone at the school, Dr. McCormack would be the last one on your list. Everyone knew this. And yet, Yacine, in his perpetual crusade for truth, had lowered his holy helmet and barreled full steam ahead. Except for my behind-the-scenes, cry-for-mercy intervention through Dr. Grossman, Yacine would've been suspended from the school indefinitely.

It had all started with Dr. McCormack's lecture on Ecclesiastes 3. The scripture when like this:

To every thing there is a season, and a time to every purpose under the heaven; A time to be born, and a time to die; a time to plant, and a time to pluck up that which is planted; A time to kill, and a time to heal; a time to break down, and a time to build up; A time to weep, and a time to laugh; a time to mourn, and a time to dance; A time to cast away stones, and a time to gather stones together; a time to embrace, and a time to refrain from embracing...

Everything had gone just fine until he reached the part where it read: *A time to love, and a time to hate; a time of war, and a time of peace.*

That's when Yacine grabbed his exegesis whip and started flogging Dr. McCormack in front of his own class.

Yacine raised his hand. "You present this scripture as having literal meaning. I know you do not intend to give that impression."

In perfect character, Dr. McCormack bristled with contempt. "Young man, I have been at this institution for nineteen years. Fortunately, no one has demonstrated the stupidity or lack of judgment to question my intent. Would you like to be the first?"

At that time, Yacine was still having trouble mastering the subtleties of the English language. And so he replied, "With no due respect for you, sir. I will be the first if it helps us to better understand the word of God."

Yacine meant *with all due respect.* But that wasn't what came out.

It was too late. Dr. McCormack's wrinkled face turned bitter orange. He scolded Yacine at the top of his voice. "Did I stutter? Did I shuffle my feet? Did I blink my eyes too many times? Did I give you any reason to believe I didn't mean what I said?"

"No, sir, indeed you did not."

"Then, what is your problem? It's all right here in black and white. You don't see an asterisk at the end of each verse. There's no exclamatory nonsense at the bottom of the page. God's word means what it says. I teach *Ecclesiastes 3* as literal because that's what it is. Is that so hard to understand?"

"It is not hard to understand. But it is impossible to accept," said Yacine. "By doing this, you have made the Bible a lie."

The room had fallen into desperate silence. We all realized this was as close to modern day blasphemy as we ever wanted to get.

"Are you calling the Holy Bible a lie?!

"No, sir, indeed I am not."

"Then, you must be calling me a liar." Dr. McCormack entertained a potential blunder that, in the minds of most students, was more egregious than the first.

At that moment, Yacine should've folded. He should've melted into a small Texas bug and sank into a dark crevice in the floor. Instead, he gripped his whip more defiantly and ordered the flogging to begin.

"Professor, I am saddened to say your literal approach to this subject does not hold true. Jesus came in love. He so died in love. He went back to the heavens to prepare a place for the ones he loves. How can you read this scripture that says there is a time to love and take it literally? By doing so you are implying there is also a time NOT to love. You are implying there is a time NOT to do what Jesus did and is still doing. And if so, you must tell me where you have found this justification in your studies."

The room suddenly became electric, to the point that if anyone moved, the static amps would polarize each other and instantly shock us into oblivion. I could tell. We all could tell. In his nineteen years at seminary, Dr. McCormack had never tasted the whip of correction, let alone from a foreigner who didn't belong in this country in the first place. He shook like a fragile leaf, sprayed by winter winds and early snow. Glassy red tears welled up in his eyes. But remarkably, none dared to slither down his face. They were too angry to fall, too proud to leave their place on high. They made no attempt to conceal his callous eyes, nor shielded the treachery of his thoughts. If the mind could be put on trial for murder, jury selection needed to begin right then and there.

Before Dr. McCormack could reply, Yacine dropped his final bombshell.

"In connection with this evidence, we cannot overlook the second part of this verse. It says, *a time of war, and a time of peace.* As human beings, we try to assign the official beginning and ending to such man-made struggles, the likes of World War II or the Six-Day War of the Jews. We say war came to this country on this date. And peace was restored on this date. But as we look beneath the veil of peace, we find the real war, by that, I mean the spiritual war between good and evil, rages on. To say there is a time of peace in the literal sense, is to ignore the ceaseless attacks by Satan and his Imps. The battle for the souls of men does not end and will not end until Jesus comes back. How, then, can you raise a literal flag of peace in the midst of war?"

It took an eternity for Dr. McCormack to unclog his gurgling throat.

"Ge-ge-get out of my class," he stammered. "Gather your belongings! Leave my presence! And don't ever come back here again!"

Though we were too frightened to bring our hands together, the applause for Yacine's courage raged in our minds. And although Dr. McCormack used his authority to remove Yacine from the classroom, he could not remove the extraordinary seeds of wisdom he had planted in our hearts.

He had brought *Ecclesiastes 3* to life as never before, and with its illumination, the invitation to search the Scripture for ourselves. It was suddenly okay to reach beyond the tired lecture notes to find the true meaning of the Word, a meaning that superseded the school's mandate for blind, subservient belief.

But in shedding our skins of innocence, we came to realize knowledge came with a price. The Bible was no longer black and white. Each verse became a deep well, requiring much research and much prayer. In the end, one could emerge from the well with a new perspective more daunting than the first.

This was the source of my anxiety. Kathy wanted her man of God to promise this was just a season, that it would soon go away. But deep inside the well of *Ecclesiastes 3* was a dark question mark, inserted there on the day of Dr. McCormack's demise. Love never ended. Neither did war. Was suffering the same way? Specifically, was our brand of suffering the same way?

You have the mark of suffering. That's what Yacine had told me. But now I needed to read the entire policy. I needed to see the small print with God's signature brand of compassion written into it. I needed to rub my fingers across the heavenly etched words in the mercy section that reassured God's people suffering was for a season, and those of us with the mark would live to see a brighter day?

Chapter Three

"*A stranger is different from both enemy and friend. A stranger is an emissary from the unknown, the placeholder of surprise, the instrument of Divine interruption, the speaker of stunning revelations. Beware, for a stranger brings his own form of gifts....*"

Evan Hodkins

*A*nother year passed. We still wallowed in the quicksand of suffering and despair. The deeper we sank, the angrier Kathy became. She was angry at God for allowing it to happen, and angry at me for following along, blindly, refusing to dump my useless faith.

It didn't help that Yacine had gone back to Africa on missionary work. The once-a-week phone calls had turned into once-a-month, then, twice a year. I had some serious questions about my so-called mark of suffering. But a perfect storm of timing, distance and misfortune had taken him out of the equation.

Kathy was slowly sinking into depression. I decided a weekend getaway might cheer her spirits. Although her mother had died of cancer, her great aunt had stepped in to raise her with the love and caring of her own child. Great Aunt Bessie Mae was still alive, residing in a senior citizen facility east of Austin.

One sunny Saturday morning in June, unable to afford a rental car, we jumped into my old reliable black Volvo s70 sedan and headed down Interstate 10.

We were thirty miles outside of Austin's city limits when the radiator started to overheat. A $120 tow truck eventually deposited our vehicle in the junky parking lot of a grumpy old shade tree mechanic just off MLK Blvd. Tired, sweaty and frustrated, we checked into a cheap motel on Pearl Street near an African/Jamaican strip center.

The mechanic promised to have the new radiator installed by dark. Otherwise, it would be Monday before he returned to the shop.

With so many failures ravishing our lives, I was determined to avoid another mishap being added to the list. We had come all the way from Houston to see her Great Aunt Bessie Mae and that's was what we were going to do.

I called a $65 taxi to take us to the Shadow Glen Senior Living facility in Bella Vista. I paid the driver an extra $20 to wait outside.

The facility was a small white brick building, half the size of a Walmart, tucked behind a clump of thick green Elm trees. The automatic glass doors slid open with a heavy clunk, allowing the pungent smell of alcohol, liniment and other disinfectants to clog our unsuspecting nostrils.

A stocky, white security guard appeared amused by our bewildered faces. What were we expecting? Didn't we know these smells were the calling cards of a fading generation, moving quietly into the night?

At the receptionist booth, we observed the ghostly movement of ten or so elderly souls, peering out from behind the smoked glass windows. They reminded me of voluntary prisoners, locked away from the new, impersonal, dog-eat-dog world by their own volition. The Bible said each generation would be worse than the previous one. Their perpetual, distrusting stares told me they wholeheartedly agreed.

"We're here to see Bessie Mae Downing," Kathy proudly announced. Her formal request brought a glint of indecision to the young receptionist's narrow green eyes. Without responding to us, she pressed a button on the switchboard.

A few seconds later, a chunky black woman with thick silver glasses came out to greet us. She carried a plexiglass clipboard, larger and fancier than that of the security guard.

"Are you members of the family?" she inquired, an unexpected seriousness in her tone.

"She's my great aunt," said Kathy, a smile of fond memories, plastered across her face. "She raised me from a little girl."

The woman glanced at her fancy clipboard, perusing a list of names. "Have you ever visited her before?"

"Not at this facility," explained Kathy.

"At any of the others?"

Kathy spiked with agitation. "I told you. She raised me from a child in Louisiana. When she moved to Port Author to live with her son, I visited her there. When her son was killed in a car accident and she moved to Freeport, I visited her there, too. I'm trying to do the same here in Austin. Is there a problem? ... Jesus!!!"

I cleared my throat. "Ma'am, we've driven all the way from Houston to see her. It wasn't the easiest trip in the world. Although, I'm sure you don't mean to, you're making us feel like aliens from another planet. All we want to do is pay her a little surprise visit and be on our way."

The woman's round face softened a bit. "I'm afraid that's not possible."

"Why not?"

"Ms Bessie passed a few days ago."

Kathy's jaws tightened. "What? That can't be right."

"I do apologize for the inquiries. It's just, we see it all the time."

"See what?" asked Kathy.

"Relatives coming out of the woodwork, hoping there's a little something in the will. They've never shown an interest before, not even a phone call or a card. But as soon as it's time to divvy up the bank account..."

"I'm not like that," defended Kathy. "I'm not looking for anything!"

"Again, I do apologize. Ms Bessie was a favorite around here. I hope you understand."

"What I understand is you shouldn't be so quick to label people before you have the facts," said Kathy. "Maybe a nice fat lawsuit would change your way of thinking."

I tugged gently at Kathy's arm. "Listen, sweetheart. The

lady did apologize. Why don't we leave it at that?"

"I can't believe you're taking her side." She snatched her arm away and stormed out of the door.

Back at the motel, I finally calmed her down. We eventually walked across the street to a cozy little Jamaican cafe with starched white table clothes and redwood floors. We enjoyed a hefty serving of bean soup and curry shrimp with eggplants, onions and zucchini. It was a rare moment of relaxation and enjoyment. Of course, it didn't last for long.

"Did you pray before we came up here?" she asked with a sweet voice of innocence.

"Yes, of course I did."

"And God still told you to come?"

"God didn't tell me anything," I admitted.

She lowered her head with sadness. "He doesn't tell us anything, does he? Not any more."

"He will one day. I'm sure of it."

She stared at me with obvious disbelief.

For a long time we sat there by the window, watching the endless parade of African locals, some, clad in brightly colored garments with long black dreadlocks swaying in the wind. Muslim women with dark hijabs covering their heads carried wicker baskets of fruit and vegetables from a local market. They laughed and chattered and hugged their children. Everyone appeared upbeat, the young teenagers, shaking their heads to the Reggae music in the background.

Kathy and I were the only ones with sad faces, the only party-poopers in the room.

As a preacher of the gospel, I couldn't ignore the irony.

All of Allah's Qur'ān-invigorated servants seemed happy and about the opportunistic business of the universe. Only the Lord's people were suffering the slings and arrows of a burnt up radiator and another failed assignment on the list. If there was a time for our feet to slip, it was indeed this time, this dreary day of escalating pain and ostracism by the God we trusted and loved.

But I had made a decision about our feet. I wasn't going to let them slip, no matter what. I turned to Kathy, still hopeful I could bring a little cheer, and somehow, salvage her day. "Why don't we do a little shopping; maybe find a few souvenirs to take back with us?"

Even the dumbest of men realized shopping was the one thing women couldn't resist.

Both, stunned and delighted by my senseless imprudence, she squinted her hazel brown eyes. "Can we afford it?"

Her question reminded me of the tow truck and the mechanic and the tight budget on which we had forced our way out of town. Every penny counted. And yet, the happiness of my sweet little spiritually bruised soul mate counted even more.

I took a deep breath, a manly breath, the kind you take when they call your number on the one yard line with five seconds left in the game. "You let me worry about that. Okay?"

We strolled down the red cobblestone sidewalk, holding hands like teenagers, licking on blue popsicles and sucking in the sweet aroma of Austin's hill country air. Passing the noisy mom-and-pop grocery stores, clothing shops and music arcades, we finally reached a small shop on the corner. The sign above the door read: Din*go's Watches, Jewelry and African Souvenirs.*

Kathy seemed amused by the chubby, brightly colored, hand-painted animal faces on the display windows. Even the lions and tigers seemed happier than us.

"Let's go in there," she said.

Once inside, we pushed pass the small crowd of chatty bargain hunters, down the dark, narrow aisles, searching the cluttered shelves for any knick-knacks or trinkets that caught our eyes. Upon reaching the counter, we had amassed a curious fortune of giraffe watches, elephant hair bracelets, an assortment of hand carved figurines, a malachite dish with matching bowls and a beautiful bone necklace that draped perfectly around Kathy's thin neck.

We were all smiles, in our minds, revisiting the glorious days in Lexington Estates when we could walk into a store and buy most anything we wanted. However, all of that came to an abrupt halt when the old man with the long beard and dark eye tallied up the cost.

"Dat will be $175," he reported in a throaty voice.

My eyeballs pushed out like white moon rocks. "Ha-how much?"

"Dis is a bargain, my brother. De bone necklace is made by de Lozi people of Botswana. At least $200 online. Get out your iPhone and do de raaasearch for yourself."

"I-ah, I don't have an iPhone."

He smiled incredulously. "Den I guess you will be forced to take de word of an old Zambezi witch doctor ... though most people would rather put dar faith in de iPhone."

"I-I-I mean, I believe you," I stammered. "But I just didn't think it would cost that much."

Kathy stretched out both hands toward the counter and shoved our entire treasure trove toward the old man's pooched stomach. "Let's just go."

"No, no," I insisted, not wanting to add another failure to the list. "You stay here. I'll be right back."

While eating at the Jamaican cafe, I had spotted a pawn shop across the street. I barged into the little green burglar-bar-riddled shack like a man being chased by wolves. The owner, a thin muscular Army type with a crew cut and black goatee, kept his hand conspicuously beneath the counter, no doubt, eager to foil my impending robbery attempt with his hair trigger release.

During my first year at the northside Kashmere Gardens church, a member had asked me to pray for him. He was going to court and needed the Lord to intervene. When the verdict came back, he won a large sum of money, much more than he had expected. He felt my prayer had something to do with it and rewarded me with a $1500 Caviar Hublot watch. It was the last remnant of our good life ... before the stars lined up. But what did it mean to me if it couldn't contribute to the happiness of the woman I loved.

I shoved the shiny black crystal in his face. "How much will you give me?"

He studied it a while. "Loan or sale?"

"Sale, I guess."

He took out a magnifying glass to examine it more thoroughly. "How much you asking?"

"How close can you get to $1500?"

He chuckled. "Brand new it's fifteen, maybe. Used like this, I'd say three hundred."

He already knew I was desperate, barging in like a runaway bull. "Make it $500 and you've got a deal."

"Three fifty is the best I can do." He handed it back to me as if it were dirt.

Of course, it wouldn't seem like dirt next week when he sold it for a $1000. But what choice did I have? I left the pawn shop with the $350, headed back to Dingo's.

Outside the store something strange caught my eye. An older woman dressed in a long black Khimar and turquoise scarf stood next to the entrance, peering through the display window. Though the scarf covered her head, strains of stiff gray hair protruded from either side of the fold, some falling unevenly across her thin, frail shoulders. With one hand, she clinched the tattered rope handles of a bulky green straw bag. With the other, she sprinkled small white granules of salt along the sidewalk in front of the door.

I assumed it was salt. It crunched beneath my feet like salt. But there was no way to ask her what it was or why she was staring through the window, sprinkling unknown particles in front of Dingo's shop. As soon as she turned and saw me coming, she hurried away.

Inside the shop, the crowd had diminished; the rhythmic African dance music had fallen into silence. Approaching the counter, I found Kathy, giggling like a little girl.

The old man appeared happily engrossed in a story about his homeland. I arrived in time to hear the tail end in which he mimicked one of his relatives: "He told dem if de lion is still out dar in de yard, we have but one choice and dat is to poison him. With dat said, he pushed his mother-in-law out the front door."

Kathy laid her head on the counter, hysterical tears, streaming down her face. She hadn't laughed that hard in years.

I waited a few seconds for her to recover, then flashed the $350. "We can get the souvenirs now."

She was still gasping for breath. "No, Rodney. I think I've changed my mind."

"Changed your mind?!" Did she understand that I had just fed a $1500 Caviar Hublot to the vultures?

"Yes, Mr. Dingo here has made us a better proposition."

"Yes," he concurred. "I think I talk too much and lose a good sale. But what de hell. You are my friends now."

"What is this proposition?" I asked.

Mr. Dingo pointed to three large brown grocery sacks on a shelf behind the counter. They were neatly stapled and taped.

"On de weekend, I offer three grab bags, filled to de brink with goodies. Some of de same things you are buying here. Only, it is an adventure because the contents will be a surprise. You pay $100 for de bag and hope for the best. I have had not so much as one complaint. De people are always happy with what dey get."

I looked at Kathy. "So you want to pay a $100 for a bag and you don't know what's inside?"

She smiled widely. "That's the whole point, Rodney. It's a surprise."

"What if we get back to Houston and it's not what you want?"

"Mr. Dino has already taken care of that."

He nodded again. "I tell her to choose a bag. Den, get the

necklace too. I will sell it to you at a very good price.

"How good?" I asked.

" It hurts me to say. And my partner will kill me. But for you, $50 and one cents. De one cents is my profit."

"You see, $150 total. That's $25 less than the original price." Kathy used her catering savvy to calculate out loud. "That's a better deal, don't you agree?"

I shrugged my shoulder. "If you say so."

Mr. Dingo's crow face sparkled with intrigue. "Now comes de big decision to rattle your brain. Which bag will you choose?"

For what seemed an eternity, Kathy scrutinized each bag. Finally, she pointed to number three.

"A very good choice, I'm sure." Mr. Dingo grabbed the bag and set it on the counter.

"I'm curious. Do you know what's inside each one?" I asked.

He smiled with boyish mischief. "Not really. My sister prepares the bags before I get here. That way, my big mouth will not spoil the surprise."

Kathy turned to survey the store. "Is she as charming as you? I'd like to meet her."

Mr. Dingo paused a brief moment, carefully choosing his words. "I think she has already left for today. She hasn't been well lately. Her mind, you know? Sometimes it comes. Sometimes it goes."

"Has she gone to see a doctor?" asked Kathy

He paused longer this time. "The things she's involved in ... no doctor can help."

We both shook our heads emphatically, as if we understood.

"But there, you can see her picture." He pointed to a photograph in a black frame, hanging over the register. He and his sister stood in the street outside a crowded meat market. Mr. Dingo looked about the same, tall, with a narrow face and a string of red beads, hanging from his neck. His sister also looked familiar ... a powdery brown face with deep wrinkles and sunken sockets of crimson eyes. And yet, I had never seen her.

"Where was it taken?" asked Kathy.

"In the Mbala District of Zambia, not far from my home village; a beautiful place it is. And the market fish in the background are fresh and sweet, plucked from the great Lake of Tanganyika."

The more I studied the photograph, the more convinced I became. The woman in the picture and the woman sprinkling salt on the sidewalk were one in the same. I was tempted to ask more about her. But the sadness of his words kept coming back to me, *Her mind, you know? Sometimes it comes. Sometimes it goes.*

The salting episode was clearly a time that it had *gone*, that is, if it was his sister's mind in the first place. I had caught only a glimpse of her small steps and fragile frame, fleeing the scene. After a long, arduous day, the Caribbean locals were all beginning to look the same. And really, what difference did it make if the creepy sidewalk christening had been carried out by her or some other demented soul? We would soon be back in Houston where the H-town, honky-tonk, Tex-Mex customs were a lot more predictable.

We left Austin with the faint orange glow of the sun, relinquishing its power to the rugged slopes and luscious green farmland. All the way back to Houston, Kathy smiled and chuckled and regurgitated the old man's funniest stories. Three years of hardship had melted into a small oasis of joy and relief. Perhaps it was only temporary. I didn't know and I didn't care. Kathy was happy again. That's all that mattered to me.

Half way home, I noticed her gawking at her mysterious grab bag. She had tucked it neatly away, in the corner of the back seat. After the third or fourth time, I finally asked, "Why don't you open it?"

"Because! That would spoil everything. I want to wait until tomorrow."

"Tomorrow?"

"Yes, after church."

"Church?" Kathy hadn't gone to church with me in months, not that she was missing anything. The large, impersonal church I had chosen was more a place of hiding than a place of worship.

"Yes. It'll be like opening our presents on Christmas Day. Aunt Bessie Mae used to say you could wish anything you wanted into your gift boxes the night before. And if you were a very good little girl, God would turn the old gift into your wish. Maybe, tonight, I'll wish for a diamond necklace or two tickets to Paris or some keys to your new church. Would you like that?"

For a split second, I turned to glance at the bag. Had I known what was inside, I would've made a wish right then and there. I would've thrown the bag out of the window and wished that tomorrow would never come.

Leander Jackie Grogan

Chapter Four

"Live joyfully with the wife whom thou lovest all the days of the life of thy vanity, which he hath given thee under the sun, all the days of thy vanity: for that is thy portion in this life...."

Ecclesiastes 9:9

People who have gone through the Great Depression die with large sums of money, hidden in their mattresses. They were there to witness the big, strong, invincible banks go under, one by one. They are quite certain it will happen again. Soldiers, coming home from war, keep guns on their night stands and under their beds. They know the enemy is out there, lurking in the darkness, just waiting for a chance to catch them off guard.

So it is with sufferers, those wheelchair-bound invalids and stroke victims and children, born blind from birth; those innocent, unsuspecting, spiritually confounded souls that have been singled out for the long haul. They anticipate the next round of suffering, reacting to it before it arrives. They develop a sixth sense that measures the intensity and potential mayhem the new suffering will bring. And then they brace themselves for one more ride through the peril and darkness, hoping for the slightest sign of relief on the other side.

Kathy and I were no different. When we awakened Sunday morning after the Austin trip to find the downstairs living room, kitchen and hallway flooded, we understood what it meant. The Austin trip had been a fluke. The ray of hope and promise of a new beginning had been a sadistic anomaly in the continued reign of terror upon our lives. The small busted pipe in the wall downstairs was like a trumpet, serenading us from heaven. It played a sad song entitled: *God Isn't Through Tormenting You Yet.*

I was the first on the scene with a mop, bucket and pair of rubber boots that leaked at the toes. I opened up the back door to swish the foot-high river into my overgrown crab grass. That's when a worrisome swarm of Greenhead flies rushed in on me. With large fluorescent green heads and angry orange eyes, they attacked with swift and painful precision, gouging a few bloody mouthfuls from my neck and shoulders before the deadly gray mist from my Raid spray can forced them back outside.

If there was a bright spot in our messy water park tragedy, it was Mr. Dingo's grab bag, resting, undisturbed, on the little round kitchen table. It had somehow been spared from the devastation, exempted in heaven as a survivor until the next round of mayhem began.

I made a quick trip to the Home Depot down the street. After replacing the leaky pipe joint, disposing of the murky water and unwanted guests, I carried the bag up to the master bedroom, our modest little 10 x 10 sleeping box with the single bay window and the ugly renter's pink and blue wallpaper on the back wall.

I wanted Kathy to know that her imaginary Christmas was still possible, that all hope had not been washed away.

She laid across our king size bed in cutoff jeans, her head, buried under a fluffy blue pillow, and hands, clutching a half empty Kleenex box. It was as far as she had gotten after peering over the banister at the swirling river below.

"I brought something for you." I announced in an artificially upbeat tone.

"I don't want it," she growled in a muffled voice. There were dresses and slips and high heel shoes scattered about the room; her obvious preparation for Sunday morning worship. But now, all of those pious thoughts had submerged beneath the flood. She was back on her boat of bitterness, riding the angry seas.

The Bible talks a lot about marriage. It specifies certain roles the husband should assume. One is to love his wife as Christ loved the church. Another is to function as the leader or head ... not dictatorially, but incorporating his wife's feelings and intimate desires into every decision he makes. Yet, somewhere near the top of the list, encrypted in the flowery language of love and devotion, is the daunting task of protecting his wife from emotional overload and the inherent uncertainties that cause her to fear.

Fear...

It shouldn't exist in the Christian universe. But it does, with shameless voracity. It lurks behind every courageous thought, every unfamiliar fork in the road and personal call to greatness. It suppresses our God-given abilities and whispers a preamble to tragedy and failure in our ear. It takes our bank accounts and family upheavals and x-ray results and transforms them into a single, sharp blade that slashes away at the days and hours and minutes of our life.

Women are inherently fearful. My older sister, Patrice, made me aware of this at an early age. They fear their size and weight and looks. They fear their vulnerability to a larger, stronger, dominate male species. They fear becoming an old maid or being traded in for a newer model. They fear becoming useless and having to live alone in their later years.

Kathy, however, harbored an even greater fear ... the fear that the kind, loving, merciful God she had known as a child was either dead or nonexistent or part of some universal conspiracy to lead mankind astray. What else could explain our three horrible years of affliction? What had we done that was so bad?

We had sought Christian counseling. But the wisest of counselors didn't have a clue. They threw out nebulous, catchall verses like *God's ways are not our ways,* or *God chastens whom he loves*, hoping the popularity and wide acceptance of such spiritual algorithms would hide their ignorance.

Who really knew the mind of God? And yet, their thick Bibles and fancy titles of *Prophet* and *Bishop* and *Apostle* created an unscrupulous obligation to make us believe they knew. In many ways, the people we talked to were cowards, unable to face their human frailties and inherent lack of understanding of what God's infinite plan was all about. They had lost the humility to say I don't know, which made them useless to us and the other spiritually baffled sojourners they claimed to serve.

In desperation, Kathy and I had discussed Allah and Buddha and Mohammed. We had taken unthinkable hypothetical journeys into the exotic teachings of Deism and Scientology. But always, we came back; back to the Christian roots that gave meaning and purpose to our lives.

Who was I fooling? I always came back. But each time she tried, a radiator would overheat or a great aunt would die or flood waters would ravage our living room floor. She didn't want to open her gift bag because only misery lurked inside. It was in there, surely it was; ready to leap out like a sly serpent to spread more poison through our already contaminated veins.

I sat down on the edge of the bed and forced the bag into the small space between us. I removed the masking tape and snapped open the stapled edges. Even before I could see what was inside, I sang a childish chorus of *oohh's* and *aahh's*.

"*Oohh*, this is unbelievable! *Aahh*, we can really use that!"

As I removed the first two items, her tear stained face slithered from beneath the soggy pillows. After a long sigh, filled with artificial contempt, she gave our mysterious trove a half-hearted glance.

Two exquisitely polished, charcoal brown African figurines lay on our white chenille bedspread. With open mouths and protruding eyes, they possessed the identical expressions of two people in pain.

"That one is you. And that one is me." My crude observation extracted a resistant smile.

She sat erectly in the bed, steering the bag away from me. "I believe Mr. Dingo gave this to me."

"Sure, sure," I said coyly. "It's just, the thing was sitting down there with no name..."

Just as Mr. Dingo had promised, the random collection proved to be well worth our gamble. Besides the figurines, Kathy found two hand painted mugs, a string of black beads, a travel pack of dominos, a zebra wallet, a silver bracelet, two fancy glass straws and a modern map of Africa with the civil war countries renamed.

It was the final item at the bottom of the bag, however, that captured our imagination; the item that neither of us could identify.

"What is it?"

She held it up to the light. "I-ah, I don't know."

I finally pried the odd contraption from her curious hands.

The small clock-like device almost defied description. It was about seven inches wide and maybe, nine or ten inches tall. It rested on a three-pronged cast iron base of dark, ornate feet, pointing in three directions. The brass base stem rose upward, like the trunk of a tree, to connect to a windmill-like silver plate. The face of the plate contained precise etchings of the sun, multiple moons and ancient hieroglyphic symbols in equal quadrants along an axis of plumb lines and dots. The entire plate was surrounded by three brass cylinders that, at the slightest touch, rotated to a different angle. At the very bottom of the plate was a long silver screw, attached to a transparent glass ball.

"Now that's weird," said Kathy, pointing to the white granules inside the glass ball.

"What?"

"Those white grains. They look just like the powdery stuff that was stuck to my shoes." She walked over to the closet to retrieve the leather sandals she had worn to Austin. She sat down beside me and flip over the soles.

"I brushed most of it off last night. But you can still see a few streaks around the edges."

My heart began to pound, though I didn't know why. I knew of the exact sidewalk christening from which the granules had come. But before I could tell her, the phone rang.

It was my sister, Patrice. I put her on speaker.

"Preacher. I tried to call you yesterday. But there was no answer. Do you still want me to come over?"

I frowned. "Come over?"

"Yes, remember you asked me a few weeks ago. You said Kathy was still acting strange and you wanted me to talk to her. Has she gotten any better?"

Why did I have the speaker on?

"I didn't say strange, Patrice."

"Okay, down in the dumps and a little weird. She doesn't want to go to church anymore, snaps a lot and has these mood swings. That's strange to me."

Kathy's head dropped to the floor.

Why did I have the speaker on?

"Look, I appreciate you following up. But this is not a good time. We had a minor catastrophe over here this morning and it'll be a while before we get things back to normal."

She grunted. "Okay, but remember I work two jobs. It's not that often I get a day off."

"I understand, Patrice. Whatever we do will be based on your schedule."

"Also, you need to talk to your niece. She won't listen. She's still running in bad company. All she knows is Scarface and Biggie-Too-Slim and Hip-hop Hank something or other. I mean, these gangster rap hoodlums are getting arrested every day."

"I will. I'll talk to her soon," I promised.

She finally hung up the phone.

I turned to Kathy. "I hope you didn't get the wrong impression."

"No, Rodney. I think it's pretty clear now. All along I thought we were going through this hell together. But now I see it's just you and your God, trying to drag me along, trying to wait until I come to my senses. How very noble of you."

She reached over to grab the last tissues from the Kleenex box.

"Look, Kathy. I'm just trying to help. You know I love you."

"What you love is being the self-righteous preacher who has some screwed up, down-in- the-dumps psycho to minister to. Well, no more of that. From now on, you need to look elsewhere for your spiritual lab rats. I'll take care of my business and you take care of yours!"

She stormed out of the room.

Down the hallway, the second bedroom was nothing more than an oversized closet, cluttered with clothes, blankets, rugs and assorted furniture; remnants from our painful downsizing after Lexington Estates. That's where Kathy fled to escape her lab rat status. That's where she hid from her self-righteous preacher-husband who spent his time broadcasting to the rest of the world her inability to cope.

All day long she stayed locked up inside, ignoring my apologetic pleas. I kept thinking she was going to come out. But she didn't. I kept thinking we were going to work it out. But we didn't.

On Monday morning, I had to leave early for work. When I returned that evening, she had dumped the blankets, rugs and furniture into the hallway and moved most of her belongings into her bedroom. I had never looked at it as her bedroom. But after a few months, I started to.

The months turned into a year. And then two years. By the time the fifth year of our continuous, self-perpetuating debacle rolled around, Kathy and I were barely talking. Without a formal discussion, we had become roommates with separate quarters, embracing schedules that relegated us to ships, passing in the night. I continued the Friday night Bible studies, which in five years, had grown to almost forty people. But during those crowded, spirit-filled sessions, Kathy stayed locked up in her room. At a certain point, I stopped making excuses for her and members of the group stop asking about her.

There was an unsettling irony. The less she talked to me, the more she talked to herself ... or somebody. Late at night I would occasionally hear strange voices coming from her room. Some mimicked her soft, alluring tone, while others were low and guttural, like the hogs mounting each other, back on my uncle's East Texas farm.

There was also this steady stream of mail: strange books and pamphlets on Transcendental Meditation, African Incantation, Astrology and Kemetic Philosophy. I knew Kathy was searching for something. But to me, she was looking in all the wrong places.

After working late one evening, I pulled into my driveway to find our electricity had been disconnected. The HL&P electric truck was just pulling away. It was a fitting end to a day when the back tire on my Volvo had blown out on the freeway, my sister's daughter had run away from home with her rapper boyfriend, and because of the Latino family's lien on my credit, my application to go full time at the Post Office had been denied.

For a brief moment I sat there, frozen in time, pitying the lifeless little wood frame house and its tormented inhabitants, now, *officially*, shrouded in darkness. The low, fatalistic horn of a distant tug boat, blasting the salty Gulf Coast air, prompted me to wonder whether it was too late to hop aboard and end all of this misery with a quick burial at sea.

Finally, I began to cry. I was suddenly a big, black, bearded buffalo, crying for all of the heartaches and disappointments and shattered dreams my choices in life had ushered in. I was crying for all of the damage I had done to my marriage; all of the faith I had wasted and the promises of God that had never come true.

You have a second chance. That's what the voice had told me. But what good was a second chance if all it did was keep you around so God could demonstrate to the angels how thoroughly and relentlessly he chastened those he loved.

I would've stayed there a million years, licking my wounds and questioning the futile purpose of my second chance in life, except for the light tapping on my passenger window. A neighbor, Miss Ella, an elderly woman with white hair and deep facial wrinkles from years of smoking, beckoned me to let down the glass.

The last thing I needed was a member of our Bible study group to see their spiritual leader, sitting there like a big crumbled cookie, sulking in defeat. But what choice did I have? I let down the window and sucked in my face.

"Preacher. Are you all right?" she gently inquired.

"Yes, yes, I'm fine."

She knew I wasn't fine, not in the least bit. I was beaten down, broken and sliding off a deep cliff.

"I saw what happened," she said. "God sent me to help."

Help.........

Perhaps it was the cleansing power of my humiliating tears, or the way the old woman's voice echoed when she said help. But suddenly, I could feel the intensity of her compassion, pressing against me like invisible fingers. She not only wanted to help, she had received her authority from the very throne of heaven. Helping was her gift, a powerful, unrelenting gift. Helping was her ... mark.

You can feel it, yes. Yacine's earliest words reverberated

through the deep cavities of my mind.

An hour later, a second electric company truck pulled up in my driveway. A younger man with a long, blonde ponytail jumped out, turned my service back on, then, drove away.

I called to thank Miss Ella, though, she did most of the talking.

"My nephew works for the light company," she said. "Maybe God put him there in advance, you think?"

I couldn't think, not with the weight of the day still bearing down on me. "I-ah, I suppose so."

"You hang in there, Preacher, you hear me?" She instructed with the heaviness of a mother, forbidding her hopeless child. "I have the whole group praying for you right now."

Many of the members were just getting to know the Lord. My scrambled, sanctimonious instincts couldn't help wondering how their childlike, baby Christian prayers looked on their way to heaven. Yacine had once told me, in the spiritual realm, a prayer was like a powerful, swirling supernaturally charged gas that radiated in multiple colors and traveled far beyond the speed of light. Some were escorted by angels of fire.

"The Comforter molds these prayers into specific shapes before they reach God's holy throne room," he said. "No man can see these shapes, for they are hidden from us. But one day soon, the great scientific minds of this world will discover their fragments. And because this phenomena will confound them, they will call it *Dark Matter*. But don't you see the irony? Prayer is not dark at all."

I didn't give much credence to Yacine's elaborate explanation. It seemed more a product of his overactive imagination than a spiritual revelation. But then, a few years later, I read an article describing a mind-boggling discovery by leading astrophysicists that explained the abnormalities in the rotational speeds of galaxies and gravitational lensing of background objects. They said all this weird stuff was being caused by invisible waves of energy, traveling through the cosmos. They called it ... *Dark Matter.*

I envisioned the shape of a lonely buffalo flying up to heaven. The way things had been going in my life, I suspected God would send out a tribe of Indians with painfully sharp arrows in their bows.

Kathy and I had an arrangement. She was responsible for the electric, gas and water bills. I was responsible for everything else. That night, when she came home from Krogers, I approached her about the delinquent bill; a debt the company said hadn't been paid in months.

She whirled around like a wild animal and glared at me. "Don't even go there, Mo#t$*f*!" She called me an unconscionable street name, the kind the rap hoodlums wouldn't even use. "If you were the man you're supposed to be, you'd be taking care of all of this #s*%#t*." Her eyes turned blood red as she stormed off to *her* bedroom.

I was paralyzed. In all the years of our marriage, she had never talked that way. I could see her lips moving. But it didn't even sound like her.

Later that night, as I tossed and turned, I heard those familiar noises again, coming from her room. First her voice, then another voice, then maybe even a third.

What was she thinking? I was still her husband. In spite of everything, I still loved her. The thought of her slipping another man into her room, right under my nose, infuriated me. I exploded from my bed and headed down the hallway. I rammed my old football shoulder against her locked bedroom door and barged in.

To my relief and bewilderment, there was no one else in the room, at least, that I could see. Even more disturbing was the fact that the loud crash had failed to awaken her.

For a long while I stood over her, reassuring myself that she was still breathing. That was when I caught a whiff of the odor, a horrible sour burnt crimson smell. It was the kind of stench that made you wonder if the sewers had backed up in the belly of hell.

As I quietly retreated toward the door, I noticed an assortment of astrology books on her night stand. The mysterious instrument from Mr. Dingo's grab bag rested prominently on the window sill, its cylinders, rotating back and forth. It's Hieroglyphic face reflected the dim light of the moon. My research had identified it as an ancient astrolabe, used in the early years of astrology. I cringed at the thought she might be involved with some Satanic cult that worshipped the stars.

The room was cold with assorted piles of clothing scattered in disarray. The dresser mirror that once reflected her silky black hair and honey-brown face had been taken down and turned toward the wall.

There was something else, something that made my heart race with fear. For the first time I could feel Kathy's mark, pressing in on me. It was the mark that now defined her. It was unmistakable. It was all encompassing. It was the unadulterated mark of ... evil.

Leander Jackie Grogan

Chapter Five

"To suffer woes which hope thinks infinite; To forgive wrongs darker than death or night; To defy power which seems omnipotent; To love, and bear; to hope till hope creates from its own wreck the thing it contemplates..."

Percy Bysshe Shelley

I had left countless messages on Yacine's cell phone and bombarded him with emails most every day. Still, no response. I desperately needed to talk to him; to anyone who could guide me through the treacherous waters that were slowly pulling me beneath the crest.

There was one other person.

After an extensive search on the internet, I finally located Dr. Roosevelt Bingham, my favorite professor back at seminary. As it turned out, he was teaching at Columbia Seminary in Decatur. In an irony of good fortune, petty politics and internal jealousy in Dallas had propelled him to greener pastures in Georgia. The new school had doubled his salary and made him a Dean.

"Mr. Rodney 'The Bull' Coleman, Texas A&M's greatest running back, ever," he recited with the deep drawl of a southern sports announcer. "Sure, I remember you. How can I help?"

I told him my whole story, right down to Kathy's sporadic behavior and the sinister voices, coming from her room.

For what seemed to be an eternity, he pondered. "First, let me tell you what I don't know. I don't know much about demonic possession. I just know it exists. Back in 2002, the late Pope John Paul II confirmed that he had been involved in three exorcisms. In fact, when he died, he was trying to get the official office of exorcists restored to the priesthood. Of course, if you don't believe a dead Pope, you should believe the Bible, which offers countless examples of people being possessed."

"But how could Kathy be possessed?" I asked. "She's a child of God ... at least she was."

"There is a scripture in the thirteenth chapter of *Matthew* that talks about separating the wheat from the tares. The profound message locked inside that chapter is that only God can look into the souls of men ... and women ... to determine whether they are true believers. A nonbeliever might act the part. But acting doesn't protect you from demonic attacks."

"Are you saying she's been faking it all this time?"

Well, Jim Jones, who did mighty spiritual works in California, led his followers over to Jonestown in Guyana and forced them to commit mass suicide. Was he faking it, all of that time?"

"I-ah, I don't know."

"Then, here's a strange tidbit to add to your confusion. For many years, the Catholic Church kept a dark secret that went by the name of *Magdalena de la Cruz*, often referred to as *Magdalen of the Cross.* Ever heard of her?"

"No, not really."

The Vatican declared her to be an honored saint. She had powerful visions that always came true. Sometime, her face would radiate with supernatural light, and hundreds of people testified to a strange public event at which she levitated in midair. Truly one of God's chosen, don't you think?"

"I-ah, I suppose so."

"What more proof do you need, Mr. Coleman? These are indisputable signs and wonders. The woman levitated in midair. Can't we agree she was a child of God?" Dr. Bingham pressed me, the way he used to do at seminary.

"I-ah suppose. Yes!"

"Wrong!" He flatly denied. "Later in life, when she became deathly ill, she confessed to a lifetime of hypocrisy and deceit. She admitted the demons inside her performed the miracles. She was found guilty by a special Spanish Inquisition and spent the rest of her life in prison."

My hands started shaking so badly, I dropped the phone.

"Mr. Coleman? Mr. Coleman?" I could hear Dr. Bingham's faint inquiry, echoing in the distance.

I retrieved the receiver from my lap. "Yes, yes, I'm here."

"Look, I'm not saying your wife is possessed," he clarified. "It could be a psychological disorder like Tourette syndrome. It causes people to have fits and act all crazy. She could be playing around with DMT, a drug that causes visual hallucinations and other psychedelic phenomena. Again, this is not my area and I don't want it to be. If anybody decides to step off into that arena, they'd better be ordained by no less than God Almighty."

"But what if she is possessed? How am I supposed to fight against powerful fallen angels that know the secrets of heaven and hell?"

"Demons are indeed powerful, Mr. Coleman. But they are not fallen angels. This is a misconception handed down during the dark ages of Christianity and perpetuated because of the restrictive nature of our official canon of scriptures. Demons are a different species of evil with completely different attributes from angels. Since I prefaced this conversation by telling you this is not my area, I won't attempt to go into detail. Just know that demons are wanderers; they seek embodiment. They want to get inside something, even if it's a filthy herd of swine on a hill. Angels, on the other hand, have their own bodies. They do their own thing."

I took a deep breath, soaking in every word. "I-ah, I see. I think I do."

"Now let me tell you about suffering, *peirasmos*, in the Greek," he continued. "It's the highest order of service to God. It has a mind of its own and a whole set of rules that go along with it."

"*Rules?*" My mind raced. I was afraid I had added to my misfortune by breaking some set of holy protocols of which I was unaware. "What rules?"

"Rule one: Don't bring suffering upon yourself. Don't cut yourself or jump off a cliff or walk on hot coals in the name of Allah."

"Why in the world would I want to do that?" I asked.

"Because of rule two: The more suffering you endure, the more powerful you become. There's a heavenly scale that measures out suffering and revelation. Through the humility that suffering brings, you are deemed worthy to handle the mysteries of God."

"I don't quite follow you."

"Remember the Apostle Peter. He was so powerful in spirit, his shadow, passing over people on the street, healed them from all manner of sickness and disease. But think about his suffering. He was whipped, jailed and crucified upside down."

A faint buzzer went off in Dr. Bingham's office. "Hold on, Mr. Coleman." After a long silence, he finally came back on the line. "I've got some people waiting. But I do want to ask you something."

"Yes?"

"In all of this suffering, have you detected a change in your cognition?"

"I'm not sure I understand your question."

"Has your eyesight improved, or has your smell or taste amplified? Are you able to do things you couldn't do before?"

I could hear Yacine's voice again, *"You can feel it, yes"*. And, in Kathy's room, I could smell it too.

"Yes, yes, I have," I finally confirmed.

"Then you're on your way," he declared, a sense of comfort in his voice. "God turns on the faucet of suffering and floats us up to a level that we can be most useful to him. Now here is the third rule and then I have to go. Are you listening, Mr. Coleman?"

I took another deep breath. "I'm listening."

"Rule three: *Trouble don't last always*. Hang in there, Mr. Coleman. At some point, God will turn your faucet off and turn your big-time blessings on."

I had spoken to Dr. Bingham in late April. Before the month

was over, Kathy had cursed out her supervisor and lost her job.

Patrice had a friend who worked at Kroger's. She explained that Kathy had been warned about the food.

"Lots of elderly people come into that Kroger's deli," she said. "They can't take a bunch of salt and pepper in their diet, not on those meds."

I knew she was telling the truth. Kathy didn't cook for me anymore. But late one night, too lazy to go out for fast food, I snuck into a pan of Kathy's leftover baked chicken. I couldn't eat it. Her once exquisite old southern recipe was drenched in salt.

What was she thinking, messing up a perfectly good recipe that all of her catering customers loved?

It was mid-June before I was able to convince her to go with me to see a marriage counselor. Only, he wasn't a marriage counselor, but a psychiatrist specializing in schizophrenia and other mental disorders.

Sitting inside his plush downtown office near Rice University's Museum district, surrounded by bookshelves stacked with advanced clinical studies and therapeutic remedies from all over the world, it had taken only fifteen minutes for Kathy to transform from a meek, troubled kitten-of-a-wife into a vicious attack dog.

"This must be some kind of joke!" She scolded the frail, paled-faced doctor. "You're trying to analyze me?! You need to be analyzing that slutty wife of yours to see which one of her boyfriends gave her syphilis. Or maybe, it was the slot machines. Yeah, that's it. The slot machines gave it to her on that trip to Vegas with the girls?"

The doctor's face reddened. His eyes bulged. He abruptly expelled us from the room.

By the time I settled her down in the lobby and returned to his office, he was in tears.

He signaled me to put away my checkbook. "How can I charge you when the axis of this session has been completely tainted by my own personal affairs?"

The $150 per hour fee was not something I looked forward to paying. But I would've paid. I would've paid $1500 an hour to make my Kathy whole again.

He whimpered. "I don't understand. How could she know this?"

"I'm sorry, so sorry." I tried to apologize.

"Just promise me this won't go any further."

I promised repeatedly, hoping to forestall any suspicions of future blackmail. "You have my word."

In the car, with a quiet, remorseful expression, she sobbed, "I'm sorry. I shouldn't have said those things."

"Why did you, Kathy? And how did you know?"

She couldn't answer.

Once inside the house, she went straight to bed.

That same evening, a few hours later, I heard a light knock on the front door. To my astonishment, Yacine was standing outside.

Thinking of all of the months … no, years he had abandoned me, I wanted to give him a piece of my mind. I wanted to call him a few choice names and recite some kind of Biblical scripture that condemned a slothful Kingdom worker to hell. But observing his fragile frame, sunken eyes and blistered skin, I couldn't muster the scorn.

He lugged a single scratched-up Samsonite through the door and flopped on our leather sofa. "My greatest apology, my friend. I have neglected my vow to you and your dear wife."

"Tell me something I don't know, Yacine."

His bony face dropped to the floor. "I didn't get your messages until I reached London a few days ago. There are no cell phones or computers in the jungle."

Yacine went on to explain that for the last year, he had retreated to a Catholic Church Missionary, and then through the unexpected providence of God, to a sacred monastery deep in the jungles of Africa for an extended period of prayer and fasting. When I asked the reason for his sabbatical, he replied vaguely, "The things I discovered at Saint Bonaventure compelled me."

"Things? What things?" I queried.

"I cannot say right now. You will just have to trust me."

I had never seen Yacine appear so troubled. Our cosmic connection was still intact, but tainted by a veil of secrecy. He was holding something back.

He quickly changed the subject. "Your situation here; how is it?"

"The same ... and worse. I've tried everything."

"I would like to see her," he requested.

"She's asleep. Maybe in the morning."

It was 3:00am in the morning when the voices began their menacing broadcast. I had given Yacine my bed and taken the sofa downstairs. Reaching the top of the stairway, I found Yacine, standing outside of Kathy's room, both hands, pressed against her door. Slowly, he walked over to me.

"I know the thing that has her. It is the demon they call *Nyambii*. The people of Zambia have worshiped him for centuries. The witch doctors make human sacrifices to him in the salt mines and seek out earthly vessels for him to inhabit."

"Salt mines?"

"It is said the salt mines were his ancient habitat before the great flood."

"And by earthly vessels, you mean … *people?*"

"Indeed. These evil spirits of darkness are very cunning. They prey on the weakest among us, leading them to slaughter like innocent lambs."

"Kathy. She is the innocent lamb, isn't she?"

"Precisely, my friend. And with this demon, the results are quite deadly. To have any chance of saving her, we must move quickly."

The next morning, with sleepless eyes and a stomach in knots, I called in sick. I kept waiting for Yacine to come downstairs to tell me what I needed to do. To pass the time, still believing in God's word, I randomly flipped through my Bible, jumping from front to back, hoping that God would lead me to a verse that would tell me what to do. His instructions were there, embedded in His holy manual. I just needed God to tell me which instructions to follow.

Anxiety and impatience finally got the best of me. I climbed the stairs to my bedroom and opened the door. There, I found Yacine surrounded by candles and incense, staring into a large marble bowl. It was filled with a dark liquid and he seemed to be in some kind of trance.

I exploded with anger. "What is this? What have you brought into my house?"

I remembered the mystical religions we studied in seminary. Scrying or gazing for enlightenment, as some called it, was a magical ritual used to try to see into the future.

A disoriented Yacine finally lifted his head. "You do not understand."

"No, YOU don't understand! This is Devil worship! I don't

want this stuff in my house."

"Don't be so intolerant!" He fired back. "I am only seeking the truth."

I held out my Bible so the white embossed lettering almost touched his face. "The truth is in this book, not in that bowl."

"It is indeed the truth, my friend. But is only a partial manifestation. It is not the complete truth."

I was petrified; these words, coming from a man of God.

"What are you saying, Yacine?! What jungle fever has taken over your mind?"

He paused a long while. Finally, he looked at my Bible. "Turn to *1 Kings 4:26*. Please read the scripture."

I quickly flipped to the Old Testament. "And Solomon had forty thousand stalls of horses for his chariots, and twelve thousand horsemen."

"Now turn to *II Chronicles 9:25*."

I read it aloud. "Solomon had four thousand stalls for horses and chariots, and twelve thousand horses, which he kept in the chariot cities and also with him in Jerusalem."

"So which is it?" he asked. "Forty thousand or four thousand?"

Before I could reply, he continued, "I know what you will say. You will say what defenders of the holy word have been saying for hundreds of years: What difference does it make? What if a careless scribe added in too many zeros to the translation? But to one seeking the truth, this contradiction can not go unresolved. One must consult the official documents of Jewish history to find the truth. This truth is outside the book you hold in your hand."

"Okay, but going to a Jewish library and pulling old records is not Devil worship; it's not divination like this thing you have going," I said.

He shook his head in frustration. "In your Bible, in the book of *Leviticus*, Chapter 16, we see the holy man, Aaron, casting lots or shooting dice to determine which of the two goats would be used for the sin offering. If you did this thing today, would not the great gatekeepers of righteous label this numerology or a system of chance, akin to divination? In *Genesis 15*, God takes Abram outside and tells him to look into the sky and count the stars. Would not the modern-day Pharisees label this stargazing and astrology?"

"That's not the point," I argued.

"That is precisely the point, my friend. We will never truly know God in all his magnificence and glory. But we must seek him on every hand. We must push aside tradition and fear and let our hearts lead the way."

"No, Yacine. We must let the word of God lead the way. This Bible says what you're doing is divination. And I don't want it in my house. You can stay. But this stuff has to go."

I stormed out of the room.

A few minutes later he had packed his bag and come down the stairs. "My plane leaves shortly."

"Okay, I'll get my keys." And then I paused, remembering his kindness to me and Kathy over the years. "Look, man. You're a good friend. I didn't mean to go off on you, but-"

"You do not have to explain," he interrupted. "And you do not have to take me to the airport." He handed me a white index card, folded twice and crinkled at the edges. Abruptly, he turned and walked out of the front door.

I followed him into the yard. "Yacine, don't be like that."

I watched him disappear down the sidewalk, taking with

him our precious friendship, and possibly, Kathy's only chance for deliverance. I knew what he was thinking. I was just like the instructors at seminary, a repressor of the truth. There was nothing I could say; nothing I could do but stand there in silence, watching his baggy blue jeans and khaki shirt fade in the distance.

Once back inside, I was reluctant ... no ... afraid to read the note he had left. No doubt, my steel blue casket was sketched out in great detail, bearing my initials. But an hour later, I found the courage. The folded note had one word written inside: *Bibliomancy*.

I had never heard of the word. I jumped on my computer to retrieve the definition.

It read: *Bibliomancy* - A form of divination using the Bible in which passages are chosen at random and the future foretold from them.

That couldn't be right.

I went to another, more trusted, respected website. It read: *Bibliomancy* - A practice first used by the Ancient Greeks whereby a person seeking spiritual insight selects a random passage from a sacred text, usually the Bible, hoping to receive instructions from God.

I flopped down on the sofa and dropped my head. Somewhere in the heavens, an angel responsible for keeping the records for all mankind had made a note:

ON THIS DAY, IN THE HOUSE OF RODNEY COLEMAN, DIVINATION WAS BEING PRACTICED WITH GREAT PASSION AND COMMITMENT, BOTH, UPSTAIRS AND DOWNSTAIRS ... ALL AT THE SAME TIME.

Chapter Six

"Through our great good fortune, in our youth our hearts were touched with fire. It was given to us to learn at the outset that life is a profound and passionate thing..."

Oliver Wendell Holmes

There's an eerie calm before a storm. One moment it's bright and sunny; the jubilant sparrows chirp in harmony as a gentle breeze slithers through the trees. The next moment the temperature drops, the wind stills and the jubilant bird choir falls into silence. A single drop of rain pelts an unsuspecting victim, perhaps, a squirrel, storing nuts, or a worm, digging a hole, or ant, clinging to a tiny blade of grass. This is the ominous warning that precedes disaster, the one-drop warning before the turbulent downpour swallows them whole.

The pelts had already begun that Thursday morning, five days after Yacine's abrupt departure. As I waited on the sidewalk outside of my house, I could see the angry squall line stretched across the horizon. A balloon-like raindrop exploded against my nose, a menacing forerunner of the fast-moving hurricane that had just entered the Gulf.

On these days, when the lightning rippled through the distant storm clouds and mother nature forced her preeminence upon humankind, I remembered the Tank ... Virgil "Tank" Brown. At six feet five inches, two hundred and fifty pounds, he earned his name by mowing down enemy combatants on the other side of the line. In high school, he was the biggest, strongest, meanest lineman in the district. He would've been the reason we won the state championship. Except, he died before we got there.

Late one afternoon, during a hot and grueling practice, a freak West Texas storm moved in. We felt the warning pelts, but Coach Ronnie ordered us to keep running the play. We heard the thunder crackle in the distance, but Coach Ronnie ordered us to keep running the play. Finally, a bolt of lightning struck a sycamore tree near the bleachers and set it ablaze. That's when he told us to make a run for it.

We stampeded toward the locker room, a few juvenile idiots, screaming and taunting the sky. That's when a second bolt came down and struck Virgil in the back. That's when a frolic in the rain became the deadly tide that bathed our young, innocent souls and opened our eyes to the instantaneity of life ... and death.

The pastor of the nearby Presbyterian Church came over to comfort us. Tall and slender with an eagle's face and eyes full of wisdom, she was the first woman pastor I had encountered. She said we had to first forgive ourselves for not heeding God's warning. She said there would be many more warnings in life, like gray hair, aching bones and teeth falling out. These things would warn us of our mortality and limited opportunity in the short span of a lifetime to make something of ourselves.

"You have to let it go," she admonished us over and over, again. "Take it as a life lesson and move on."

Although my eleventh grade English teacher had transformed me into the resident wordsmith, I didn't understand why she placed so much emphasis on the last part, the part about letting it go. But Coach Ronnie did.

Still, her words were not enough to keep him from committing suicide a few weeks after we lost the state championship by an extra point. Everyone thought it was the game. But as I grew older and understood the true meaning of her words, I realized it wasn't the game, but the decision he had made leading up to the game, the decision that submerged him in unshakable guilt, the decision that snuff out a young life to which, in him, God had entrusted.

That morning, when the supersized raindrop slammed against my nose and the distant thunder clamored in my ear, a tragic life lesson reared its ugly head. We had our warning. It was time to abandon the silent call of the bird choir and go back inside.

I say we because just up the sidewalk, half a block away, I spotted Betty Frazier, a recently retired nurse and member of the Bible study group, out for a morning walk with her dog. In reality, it was more a ride than a walk. Clutching the thick rubber handles of her red Avenger all-electric Medicaid scooters, she zipped toward me like a one-woman motorcycle gang.

"Good morning Preacher. Why aren't you at work?" Betty always had a lot of questions. Some were about the Bible and the wretched state of society. But mostly, they centered on finding her a new husband.

"I called in today. Not feeling well." I couldn't tell her the voices from Kathy's room had grown louder and more disconcerting, keeping me up most of the night.

As I spoke, her tiny brown Chihuahua started to bark like crazy.

"Oh, Putts, now, now. I thought we were friends." I spoke in a soft, monotone voice, trying to calm him down. The more I observed him, however, I realized he wasn't looking at me. He was barking at the second floor window overlooking the driveway.

"What room is that?" asked Betty, pointing to the same window.

"It's our second bedroom."

"Putts doesn't like that window," she revealed. "Any cats or birds?"

"No. Just a small junky space, mostly for storage."

And estranged wives that cry out in the night, I thought to myself.

"I think Putts sees more than storage," she said. "But he can't say."

All that Putts failed to say, he made up in his annoying, ever persistent barking.

She continued. "I do wish he could talk. He could keep me company until I met someone special. Since Harvey died, I get lonely sometimes. And you know how hard it is to meet someone special, especially at my age."

A deafening clap of thunder sent shock waves through the sky.

"I don't think Harvey would like you being out in this weather," I surmised. "That overcast is moving in pretty quickly. Could be dangerous if you're caught outside."

"Why are you standing out here, preacher?"

Before I could answer, Putts jerked his chain from her

wrinkled hand and ran into the middle of the yard. He peered up at the window, barking ferociously.

Suddenly, a gust of wind picked up my aluminum trash can and slammed it into Putts' tiny, noisy frame. With a loud, injured squeal, he dashed toward the scooter and leaped into Betty's lap. A second gust blew the trash can into the street where a passing pickup truck smashed it to smithereens.

Betty clutched the trembling Chihuahua in her fleshy arms. "Oh my God, Putts! Are you all right?"

Except for a mild whimper, the dog uttered not a sound.

"I'm so sorry, Betty. Yesterday was trash day. I should've put that can away."

"It's not your fault, Preacher. Like you said, this weather is getting crazy. We both need to get inside. And my brave little darling too. Come on, Puttcy Puttcy Poo."

As she turned her scooter around and headed down the sidewalk, a shiny white Escalade with black tinted windows and sparkling chrome wheels, pulled into my driveway. The music was almost as loud as the thunder. The smell of marijuana permeated the air.

I already knew who was inside; my reason for being out there in the first place; my reason for still standing there beyond the one-drop warning God had so mercifully supplied.

Patrice had convinced her daughter to come over to talk to me. A bit puzzled about the location, she had called on her cell so I could keep an eye out for her.

"I'm not alone," she had alerted me in an unyielding tone. "If you have a problem with that, you need to let me know now."

With such an arrogant proclamation, my first thought was to tell her never mind. But Patrice had been so gracious to us since we moved to Houston. And the girl was my niece.

The girl...

I needed to start calling her by her name ... Shameeka.

I didn't like that name. Back in Dallas, all the Shameeka's I knew were hookers and drug heads. Of course, it was too late to rename her. I just prayed it wasn't too late to remold her as well.

Observing me standing there in the driveway, braving the incessant drizzle, I expected her to jump out and come inside. Instead, the rear door opened and a figure, who I suspected was King Kong's younger brother, got out. He was adorned in baggy designer jeans, $500 tennis shoes, dark shades and multiple gold chains. His right hand was concealed beneath his "Rap or Crap" sweatshirt. But the protruding bulge left no doubt of the large weapon, buried in his huge hands.

Without the slightest greeting or eye contact, he surveyed the driveway, the house, the interior of my Volvo and surrounding yards. Finally, he nodded to the inhabitants inside the black tint.

Shameeka stepped out in a bright blue mini skirt, silver bracelets, adorning her ankles and wrists. Her hair showcased multiple streaks of blonde, and the blue gloss, smeared across her thick lips, matched her skimpy dress.

"What's up, Uncle Rodney?" She greeted me with a big hug.

"It's all good." I eyeballed her, then the Escalade. "Or so it seems to be."

The passenger door opened. A young man in his early 20s with tattoos, dreadlocks and sagging pants, strolled between the two vehicles and extended his hand. "Johnnie D in da house, baby. Peace and love to you."

"Sa-same to you." I couldn't keep up with the multiple hand

shakes, slaps and dapps. Still, I offered a cordial smile.

"You da preacher man I take it? Heard a-lotta soulful thangs about you."

I glanced at King Kong's younger brother, his hand still resting uneasily beneath his shirt. "Apparently their assessment of me wasn't too convincing."

He smiled coyly. "Oh, don't mind Tiny-Bone, here. He's just the insurance man, knowemsayin'?"

"Insurance? I'm afraid I don't understand."

"Naw, you wouldn't. It's a East Coast, West Coast, South Coast thang, knowemsayin'? I'm getting ready to sign a $5,000,000 contract with some white boys out of LA. Lotta people don't like that. Lotta people would like to send me to the party with Tupac and Biggie Smalls. But I ain't quite ready to go, knowemsayin'? That's where Tiny-Bone comes in."

As he spoke, the drizzle slowly intensified. The thunder boomed over our heads.

"Why don't we go inside," I offered. "What I have to say won't take very long and there's no need of us getting soaked in the process."

Tiny-Bone entered first, his big suspicious eyes, roaming the hallway, kitchen and staircase. Though, the three of us sat around a coffee table in the living room, Tiny-Bone removed a chair from the kitchen table and positioned himself by the front door.

After retrieving them some bottled water from the refrigerator, I began with a short prayer. I wanted to follow up by reading a scripture. But my large black Bible was nowhere to be found. Knowing Shameeka was on her way, I had intentionally left it on the coffee table. Now it was gone.

Still, I knew the essence of the Scripture I wanted to share: *When I was a child, I spake as a child and thought as a child, and acted as a child. But when I became a man, I put away childish things...*

This is what I recited to them ... or, at least, tried. Halfway through my recitation, the television came on by itself. It flipped through several channels until it landed on a concert performance by some rap group.

Shameeka pointed excitedly toward the screen. "That's Baby Shakaa and Lil'Man."

Johnnie D offered a modest nod. "I'm feelin' Lil'Man. But she ain't all that."

Surely, someone was sitting on the remote control.

That's what I thought until I spotted it on the table near my computer.

I walked over, grabbed the remote and turned off the television.

"Awwh come on, Uncle Rodney. That's one of my favorite songs," she whined.

"You've got plenty of time to listen to this Shakka-butt or other. Right now, I'm trying to give you some information that's going to help you for years to come."

I sat back down on the sofa. That's when the radio in the kitchen came on. It was playing a vulgar rap tune from a station called *The Box.*

Johnnie D's face lit up. "That's Pimp C, my first mentor. Took me under his wings, knowemsayin'? How'd you do that, Preacher? How'd you bring the master into our presence like that?"

Before I could answer, the television came back on, then the cake mixer, then the microwave oven which started to ding over and over, again. Down the hallway, the toilet had started to overflow. Dirty water streamed from beneath the door. Finally, the lights went out.

I had paid the electric company. I knew the electricity hadn't been disconnected because the television and microwave and all the other appliances continued to scream.

Tiny-Bone stood up with a wild look on his face, his 357 Magnum in plain sight. "Let's get up outta here, baby. Something ain't right."

They all turned toward the door. That's when we saw it. Through the picture glass window, we observed both the Escalade and Volvo inching slowly toward the street. They were like an unauthorized train, neither hooked together nor touching, yet, moving in concert, down the slick driveway. A deep voice from the top of the stairway echoed through the darkened room. "Steve."

Johnnie D glared at Shameeka. "Who the hell is Steve?!"

The years of loud music had distorted their young ears. But even above the infamous concert being performed by the television, microwave and cake mixer, I heard the voice with ominous clarity. It didn't say Steve. It said ... *LEAVE!*

Without the benefit of clarity, Tiny-Bone rumbled outside, into the drizzle, down the driveway, and using his own remote, started the Escalade. By the time Johnnie D and Shameeka hopped in, the spinning back tires had transformed a large puddle of water into a smoky gray mist.

The moment the Escalade disappeared around the corner, the lights came back on. One by one, the appliances fell into silence. Even more mind boggling was the reappearance of my Bible. It now rested on the coffee table where I had left it, seemly undisturbed.

God had given me a one-drop warning ... that mother nature was on the rampage and mere humans needed to find a place to hide. But now came a second warning, a more diabolical message that signaled a changing of the guard. The little wood frame house no longer belonged to preacher/husband Rodney Coleman and his estranged wife. It had a new owner. It was now in the hands of ... evil.

I stood there in the living room, exploring my options. Who was I kidding? I had no options. Kathy had fallen into a deep black hole. The rent was past due. My supervisor had warned me if I missed another day, I would be put on probation. I didn't have the money or the will to move out and leave Kathy behind. And yet, I had lost the courage to stay.

That's when the phone rang.

Yacine's familiar voice bolted through the receiver. "We could spend our time on the appropriate apologies, my friend. But I believe we have a more pressing matter."

"Yes, yes, more than you could imagine."

"I have made a strong appeal to Father Devann about our situation," he reported. "He has agreed to come to Houston to perform the exorcism."

Exorcism? I envisioned my beautiful wife caught up in some kind of barbaric ritual.

"Whhh-wait a minute," I stammered. "Is that our only option?"

"Yes. And it must be done tomorrow night, at midnight."

"Tomorrow?" Earlier that morning, I had watched the local newscasters, updating the coordinates of the approaching hurricane. "You do know there's a storm coming in."

"Let us be honest with each other, my friend. Your storm has already arrived."

I paused for a long moment, slowly surrendering to his painful truth. Finally, I asked, "Why midnight?"

"Because, my friend, that is the beginning of the day when the sun will stand still."

Chapter Seven

"For though we walk in the flesh, we do not war after the flesh: For the weapons of our warfare are not carnal, but mighty through God to the pulling down of strong holds; / Casting down imaginations, and every high thing that exalteth itself against the knowledge of God...."

Apostle Paul of Tarsus

By the time Yacine and Father Devann arrived the following afternoon, the entire city had transformed into a beehive of terror. Panic-stricken shoppers scrambled from store to store scavenging batteries and candles and plywood to board up their windows. One by one, businesses and schools closed, allowing employees and students precious lead time to hunker down for what would surely be the worst disaster in the city's history.

Except for a fifteen minute trip to the corner pet store, I had been careful not to stray too far from home. Yacine had given me explicit instructions.

"In her condition, she will have knowledge of certain things," he warned. "If she discovers we are coming, she might try to run away."

Every few hours I had looked in on her, only to find her fast asleep. Fortunately, the uneventful bed checks had not deterred my preliminary research on the computer downstairs.

I discovered that June 21st marked the beginning of the summer solstice, a Latin word meaning *cause to stand still.* It was the day the sun reached its maximum elevation over the Northern Hemisphere; the day with the greatest number of daylight hours, and according to Yacine, the day when evil spirits and demonic powers of darkness were most vulnerable.

I was encouraged to see how many times Father Devann's name came up during my Google searches on exorcism and the expulsion of evil spirits. As a young friar, devoted to service in the poverty-stricken countryside of Ireland, he had worked his way up the ranks to become an iconic figure in the priesthood and leading expert in the field of exorcism. He had performed over two hundred official rites in the United States alone.

He was the legendary Franciscan priest under which Yacine had studied for years. And yet, as they walk through my front door, lugging four huge metal suitcases, they seemed worlds apart. Yacine still appeared fragile and underweight from his months of fasting in the jungle. Father Devann, a hulking six foot four, two hundred and ninety pound giant, with wild eyes and a ruddy face, seemed hardened and ready for war.

"Thank you so much for coming." I greeted them with an outstretched hand. They walk right past me and dumped their suitcases on the floor. I continued to extend my hospitality, trying to lighten their somber mood. "When I first saw you walking up the driveway, I thought Father Devann was the University of Texas linebacker that cracked my collar bone, and was coming here to finish the job."

They didn't laugh at my attempted humor. They didn't hear me at all. Father Devann had walked over to my framed maroon and white Texas A&M football jersey, hanging on the wall. "This must come down."

Yacine turned to see the fury, building in my eyes.

"It is because of the number," he explained.

"What's wrong with 18?" I asked. This was the number that had carried me through a record-breaking season.

"It is a derivative of 6, such as 6 plus 6 plus 6," he continued. "Anything with 3 or 6 must come down."

I lifted the frame from the wall and slid it into a storage closet. "Anything else?"

Yacine pointed to his gift of many years ago, the gold plated cross, hanging over the fireplace. "The cross must come down also. We will need it in our service."

I retrieved a stepladder from the same storage closet and began my begrudging ascent.

It didn't feel right, taking down the cross. That cross was a symbol of God's love for his people, a reminder of Jesus' victory over sin and death. That cross had been through hundreds of Bible studies and even generated a debate with a visiting Jehovah's Witness about the Babylonian worshipers of the cross, a debate that had ultimately saved his soul. There wasn't much virtue left in the old wood frame house. Didn't they have another cross they could use?

Yacine saw the troubled look on my face. He seemed to be

reading my mind.

"Each administration is subservient to another administration," he said. This is a critical thing you must remember throughout our ordeal."

I knew he was trying to tell me something; just as the preacher woman from the Presbyterian Church had tried. But I didn't get it. Before I could ask him more about it, Father Devann started to laugh.

Standing in the kitchen, peering up at the top shelf of the food pantry, he had found something that amused him. He finally pulled down six boxes of Morton's granulated salt.

"This must go," he ordered. "Pour it down the kludgie at once!"

Yacine hurried over, took the boxes from his large hands and stepped into the hallway bathroom. He flushed a few times, then reappeared with five empty boxes. "Where is your trash can?"

"Why--"

"Because the demon, Nyambii, feasts on salt," he answered before I could ask. "Now, your trash can, my friend. Where is it?"

"Under a pickup truck."

Yacine appeared bewildered.

"Here." I took the boxes from him. "There's a trash bag in the garage."

Father Devann turned to me as if recognizing my presence for the first time. "What have you been eating?"

"Nothing!" I defended. "Yacine told me to fast."

For a while he studied my face, as if determining whether I was telling the truth. Then, he looked at Yacine. "Give him the holy water and make sure he drinks it all."

When I returned from the garage, Yacine had opened one of the suitcases. It was protected by so many latches and combination locks; it could've easily contained the codes to an atomic bomb. He removed seven blue canisters of water. "You must drink all seven before the service so that your body will be purified."

I immediately guzzled two down and cradled a third in my hand. That's when we heard the loud, gurgling scream, coming from Kathy's room.

As if using x-ray vision to peer into her room, Father Devann looked up toward the ceiling. "He knows we're here."

"Whhh-what does that mean?" I nervously inquired.

"It means that as we prepare for him, he will be preparing for us." Father Devann walked down the hallway to the bathroom and shut the door.

With Father Devann out of the room, Yacine reached into his leather satchel to pull out a brown envelope. He took a deep breath before speaking.

"We have a great journey ahead of us, my friend. I don't know how all of this will turn out. But you must take this and put it away, somewhere safe. Open it, only when this is behind us."

I took the envelope and placed it in the freezer, a safe haven for valuables and the few emergency dollars we had hidden around the house. Then, I looked back at Yacine. "You think all of this is going to work?"

Yacine gazed out of the window at the hapless tree limbs, whipping violently against the house. "When the storm is raging, we who believe must trust in God. And we must trust each other. Then, at least we have a fighting chance."

When Father Devann returned, they opened the remaining

suitcases. They pulled the kitchen table into the living room, using it as the center of an elaborate staging area. Slowly and methodically, they began to assemble an arsenal of spiritual weapons of which I had never seen.

Five hours later, at exactly 10pm, the assortment was complete. The little round breakfast table sagged with Bibles and metals and crosses. There were, among other items, three kinds of holy waters, sacred wine, shackles with sterling silver chains, ancient relics from the Vatican and white towels, soaked in the Holy Rivers of Bethany.

Though, I marveled at the collect, I had not been allowed to touch any of the items.

"You must be consecrated first," explained Yacine. "This will begin at 10:22pm sharp."

I couldn't help asking, "Why 10:22pm?"

"Have you never read about the ten horns in the Book of Daniel?" growled Father Devann. "Ten represents God's perfect order before the Age of Aquarius. Twenty-two is the holy number of God's Begotten Perfection."

He rose from his seat and head toward the restroom on another blue canister run. A few feet down the hallway, he laughed cynically to himself. "Seminary, these days, is but a waste of time."

There it is again, I thought to myself. Another condescending remark from the so-called holy man of God.

In my old Dallas street days, I would've punched him out. But we were new creatures in Christ. Love, compassion and forgiveness was the order of the day ... wasn't it?

I finally asked Yacine. "Is he like this all the time?"

"The situation is very complicated," he sadly reported.

"More than you could ever imagine."

Father Devann returned from the restroom dressed in a black surplice, both shoulders embroidered with tentacles of gold. He donned a purple stole around his neck and a single white silk glove on his right hand. His soft sole Oxfords were gone, replaced by black, knee-high boots, tipped in pure gold. With the deep voice of authority he declared, "The time has come."

At that moment, the whole house shook from the storm's angry winds. A huge tree limb crashed against the back door. Shattered glass splattered the driveway as another street light crashed to the ground down.

Yacine reached under the table to hand me a pair of the gold-plated boots. "You must wear these at all times. The demon we face enters through the toes."

I suddenly caught a flash of Kathy's leather sandals, covered with salt.

With our boots tightly laced, Yacine and I stood by the table. Father Devann draped us with individual purple stoles, a sterling silver bracelet and a gold chain carrying the *Metal of St Benedict.* Slowly, he began to sprinkle us with holy water.

"All-powerful God, pardon all the sins of your unworthy servants. Give them constant faith and protection so that, armed with the power of your holy strength, they can attack this deceitful and evil spirit in confidence and security."

With his huge, forceful index finger, he pressed the sign of the cross onto our foreheads. He resumed showering us with the water. "Speak now and declare your allegiance to Almighty God. Do you accept the Father, the Son and the Holy Spirit as your God? Do you surrender all to him? Do you accept this glorious task he has put before you? If so, let it be known by saying, I do."

Yacine and I responded simultaneously. "I do."

"Then, may Christ, the Virgin Mary and all the saints of God be with you in this endeavor so that in the end, hell will be overrun and heaven will prevail forever and ever, Amen."

Whether it was his voice powering over us or the cool, purified droplets, slowly seeping beneath my skin, something was happening, a growing sensation inside me, like liquid fire spreading through my veins. Although, I couldn't put my hand on it, I realized I was somehow, stronger than before. The howling wind and unremitting rain were not as frightening. More importantly, my fear for Kathy's future had begun to subside.

Father Devann looked at me with fiery eyes. "Where are the turtle doves?"

I went into the garage to retrieve the three white pigeons Yacine had instructed me to buy at the pet store. I set their three cages on the floor near the table.

Father Devann sprinkled each bird in each cage with holy water. "May these sacrificial instruments be found pleasing in God's sight. May they serve the purpose for which they were intended before the foundations of the world."

He then covered each cage with the towels from the Holy Rivers of Bethany.

Fortunately, my cosmic connection with Yacine was still intact. Without asking about the three pigeons, he explained, "Nyambii is not one demon, but three in one. Once expelled, he will seek out a host in which to dwell."

We prayed and read scriptures for almost an hour. Then, at 11:40pm, Father Devann shouted in a loud voice, "Prepare the sacred tray."

Yacine screwed together two halves of a three foot silver tray. He then loaded most of the items from the table onto the tray. He handed me the shackles, four Bibles and the gold-plated cross, the one he had given us on our wedding anniversary. Then, he pointed to the cages. "Once we have placed these instruments outside her room, you must come back for the cages. Understood?"

At 11:50pm, carrying only the red leather, 80-page *Rituale Romanum,* the official exorcism manual, Father Devann led us up the staircase and down the hallway to Kathy's bedroom door. Just as Yacine had instructed, I deposited the shackles, Bibles and cross by her door and headed back downstairs for the cages.

Suddenly, I heard someone pounding on my front door. I was stunned to find Miss Ella and several members of the Bible study group, standing outside.

"What, in God's name, are you doing out in this weather?" I asked.

As I shouted through my screen door, a neighbor's lawn chair sailed over their heads and crashed into the side of the house. I quickly opened the door and ushered them into the living room.

Miss Ella was rain-soaked and trembling. Bobby and Stella Johnson stood behind her, wiping the face of their two-year old son. Betty Frazier frantically checked the pockets of her raincoat, eventually lifting a disoriented Putts to her chin. Skip, the waterfront drunk, coughed from a bad cold, as Hanna, the librarian, dried the lenses of her thick glasses. All the while, Mr. Floyd, Miss Ella's gray-haired, invalid brother, slowly relinquished his slippery grip on his metal walker. By the time I grabbed him, he was half way to the floor.

I sat him down in a nearby armchair, then fetched some clean towels from the hallway closet to dry them off.

"I guess we got a little antsy," said Miss Ella.

"No! Downright scared." Mr. Floyd was a former oilman who didn't mince words.

"Yes, we were frightened," she finally confessed. "We had decided to gather at my house to pray through the storm. But when the lights went out, we didn't know what to do."

"We looked across the street and saw your lights were still on," Stella Johnson reported. "Did you know the whole neighborhood is pitch-black, except for your side of the street?"

Before I could answer, Yacine stuck his head over the banister. "My friend, we are running out of time."

"Who is that man?" Betty Frazier questioned.

"Did we catch you at a bad time, Preacher?" inquired Miss Ella, fixated on the St. Benedict medal around my neck.

Before I could answer, Yacine scurried down the stairs. He pulled me to the side and whispered, "This is a very critical moment, my friend. We do not need any distractions."

Miss Ella overheard him. "We didn't mean to barge in on you, Preacher. Maybe we should go."

Suddenly, the little wood frame house shook violently against the wind.

"No," I declared.

At that moment I realized I had become more to them than just a Friday night Bible study instructor. I was the closest thing they had to a pastor ... No. I was their pastor and they were my flock. There was no way I was going to put them out to be swallowed up by a killer storm.

I turned to the group. "How many are here?"

"Ten," replied Stella Johnson.

"That's a perfect number I've been told."

Yacine cringed. "You will let them remain?"

"Ten additional prayer warriors? Why wouldn't I?"

I turned to my *help* specialist. "Miss Ella, I'm putting you in charge. Don't let anybody touch anything on that table or in those metal cases. You understand."

She nodded affirmatively.

"Look in the kitchen cabinet. Find candles for everyone. Do what you set out to do. Pray. Pray like you've never prayed before."

"What shall we pray for, Preacher?" she inquired.

I took a deep breath, trying to envision the shapes their tender cries for mercy should take. The words suddenly came. "Pray for a bird choir that sings melodious songs of victory. Pray that an old wounded buffalo will be renewed in strength. Pray that the sun will stand still long enough to shine a glorious light from heaven. Pray that evil will be forced to retreat to the darkest corner of hell."

I grabbed the three cages and followed Yacine up the stairs.

Leander Jackie Grogan

Chapter Eight

"Life is, in fact, a battle. Evil is insolent and strong: beauty, enchanting but rare; goodness very apt to be weak; folly very apt to be defiant; wickedness to carry the day; imbeciles to be in great places, people of sense in small, and mankind generally unhappy. But the world as it stands is no illusion, no phantasm, no evil dream of a night; we wake up to it again forever and ever; we can neither forget it nor deny it nor dispense with it...."

Henry James

When we entered the room, it was cold, dark, and reeking with an ungodly stench. The bed was empty. Kathy was nowhere to be found.

Meticulously, Father Devann surveyed the sacred tray for a small black, drawstring pouch. Reaching inside, he showered the room with dried salt from the Dead Sea. To my amazement, most of the granules stuck like darts against the closet door.

"She is there," announced Father Devann.

When we pulled open the door, the strong smell of urine

flooded our noses. Kathy lurched from the darkness, engulfed by a swarm of Greenhead flies. Fending off their ferocious attack, we missed the fully heated electric travel iron in her hand. With split-second timing, she scorched Yacine's neck and whacked me in the chest. A few seconds later, she unleashed a torrent of watery green vomit into Father Devann's face.

One spray from an unmarked white aerosol can flooded the air with a heavy gray mist. Immediately, even before Father Devann could return the can to the tray, the entire swarm of flies dropped dead to the floor.

It took our combined strength to drag her from the closet and shackle her to the thick brass bed railing. Stretched out across the sheets in a missionary position, her soiled blue gown kept creeping above her waist. With an instinctive sense of discretion, I kept trying to pull it down. Each time, however, she flooded me with a volley of green spit.

Finally, Father Devann shouted, "Do not be distracted by the tricks of the devil. He will use your weakness to his advantage."

She screamed with terror as he doused her with a handful of holy water. "I exhort you, Most Unclean Spirit! Reveal your origin. Show us your instruments of seduction. I demand this in the name of Almighty God."

He grabbed Kathy by her long hair and forced her to look at two small ruby-studded crosses in his hand. She cried out, even louder this time.

As her hysterical protest reached its peak, Mr. Dingo's ancient bronze astrolabe fell off the window seal, onto the floor.

Father Devann pointed to the old gadget, its brass cylinders still swaying back and forth. "This is the instrument of seduction. Neutralize it!"

Yacine grabbed a different colored bottle of holy water, a dark blue liquid, and poured it over the astrolabe. He covered it with a towel from the Rivers of Bethany.

"I know who you are Most Unclean Spirit! You are Nyambii, three times cursed, stronger than man, but weaker than God. I exorcise you in the name of the Father, Son and Holy Spirit. Be ye uprooted and expelled from this beautiful Creature of God."

As though he were branding a wild Texas calf, he pressed his metal of St. Benedict into her jaw. A cloudy gray mist rose from her pores.

"Depart from us, Oh Serpent of Evil! This is no longer your dwelling place. You cannot make a mockery of God."

Kathy looked at me with pitiful crocodile eyes. "They're hurting me, Rodney. I love you, Rodney. Are you going to let them hurt me?"

Instinctively, I moved forward. But Yacine grabbed my arm. "She is not the one saying this. You must realize it is a ploy."

Father Devann opened his big, black tattered Bible and began to read. "And when he saw Jesus from a distance, he ran and fell on his knees in front of him. He shouted at the top of his voice, What do you want with me, Jesus, Son of the Most High God? Swear to God that you won't torture me! For Jesus had said to him, Come out of this man, you evil spirit!"

As he read with increasing vigor, Kathy's eyes rolled back in her head. She groaned and growled and squirmed. Undeterred by her pleas, Yacine sprinkled her with more holy water.

Father Devann continued reading from his Bible. "Then Jesus asked him, What is your name? My name is Legion, he replied, for we are many. And he begged Jesus again and again not to send them out of the area. A large herd of pigs was feeding on the nearby hillside. The demons begged Jesus, Send us among the pigs; allow us to go into them. He gave them permission, and the evil spirits came out and went into the pigs. The herd, about two thousand in number, rushed down the steep bank into the lake and was drowned."

Father Devann stepped over to the sacred tray and removed the last relic. It was a golden Pyx with a silver Crucifix engraved on the front. It reminded me of my grandfather's old pocket watch, but thicker, and without the chain.

Yacine whispered, "It was given by the Pope. There may be seven of those in the whole world."

Father Devann opened the Pyx and began to sprinkle its contents over Kathy's entire body.

"What's in there?" I inquired.

"Shavings of gold, my friend; It is believed from bricks Solomon used to build God's temple."

"Silence!" Father Devann ordered as the yellow granules floated down from his hand. And then he began a long Latin chant: *Exorcizamus te, omnis immundus spiritus, omnis satanica potestas, omnis incursio infernalis adversarii....*

Without ceasing, he read ten pages from the *Rituale Romanum*, the official exorcism manual:

"Blessed Lord and Father, almighty and everlasting God, who is, who was, who ever shall be, whose beginning is unknown, whose end is inconceivable. We humbly implore you on behalf of this servant of yours whom you have freed from the shackles of error; graciously heed her as she lies low before you at the well of cleansing where one is born over again by water and the Holy Spirit. May she adorn your spotless robe and thus become worthy of serving you, our God..."

And then he resumed his Latin chant.

And then another ten pages, followed by the chant.

"Hear, accursed *Nyambii*, for I adjure you in the name of the infinite God and His Son, Jesus Christ, our Savior, to flee in trembling and groaning, for you and your envy are vanquished. May you have nothing in common with this servants of God, whose thoughts are already of heaven, and who is determined to renounce both you and your world and to overcome you and so win a blessed and immortal reward..."

At the end of the chant, he cried out, "Almighty God, whose nature is ever merciful and forgiving, accept our prayer that this servant of yours, bound by the fetters of sin, may be pardoned by your loving kindness. I beg thee, Oh God; release her from the grasp of this Evil One. Let the Great Seducer be humiliated and cast down. Show your awesome power in this hour, this minute, this second in the name of the Father, Son and Holy Spirit!"

Suddenly, Kathy screamed, not in one voice, but three. The room shook. My ears pop, as though I were in an airplane. A dark, frigid wind passed through me, through us all, on its way to the cages.

All three pigeons began to flutter and squawk. Then, in an instant, the whole room fell into an eerie silence.

I looked at Kathy. Her eyes slowly opened. A sense of panic quickly engulfed her as she struggled to escape the shackles.

"It's okay, darling. Relax." I started toward her. Father Devann, however, stretched out his arm to block me. He reached over to press his metal of St Benedict against her forehead, carefully gauging her tender response.

"God of heaven and earth, God of the angels and archangels, God of the patriarchs and prophets, God of the apostles and martyrs, God of the confessors and virgins, God of all the devout; God whom every tongue praises and before whom all bend the knee, in heaven, on earth, and in the depths; I call on you, Lord, to watch over this servant of yours in like manner and lead her in your kindness to the grace of your baptism; through Christ our Lord. Amen."

An eternity passed before he nodded for me to proceed.

Yacine unlocked the shackle, slowly, deliberately, as if unconvinced she had been restored. But I knew it was my Kathy. I could feel her mark. It was the mark of devotion and love.

For a long time, I sat on the side of the bed, holding her tightly in my arms. Finally, I looked into her eyes. "How do you feel?"

She thought for a while. "I feel like I've caused you a lot of pain."

"You better believe you have. But don't worry. I'll give you a chance to make it all up."

She smiled, a bright smile, a hopeful smile I had not seen in years. I grabbed a hand full of clothes from her dresser drawer and escorted her into the hallway. Miss Ella was already standing at the top of the stairs.

"I heard noises," she reported. "I didn't know if..."

"I'll explain everything later," I said. "Right now, I need you to take her into my bedroom."

"*Your* bedroom?" She tried to clarify.

"That master bedroom down the hall, Miss Ella. Help her with a hot bath. Help her to get cleaned up. Can you do that for me, Miss Ella?"

She smiled warmly. "It would be my pleasure."

They walked a few steps down the hall before she turned

back. "The radio said the worst of the storm has moved down the coast to Corpus Christi. We're not out of the woods, but we're on our way."

I gazed into Kathy's weary but hopeful eyes. "Yes we are, Miss Ella ... on our way indeed."

I turned to head back into Kathy's room. Yacine had just finished pouring three small jiggers of ritual wine from an ancient bronze Yu. He handed one glass to Father Devann, another to me, and kept one for himself.

Father Devann held his glass high. "In *1st Timothy 5*, it says a little wine is good for the belly."

"Especially, after God has given us such a wonderful victory," added Yacine.

"Amen to that," I chimed in.

"Then let us drink to God's victory over evil," commanded Father Devann.

We guzzled our drinks to the last drop.

"So the demon is in the pigeons?" I asked, cautiously eyeing the silent cages.

Yacine walked over to remove the towels. All three pigeons were dead, their beautiful white feathers, charred by a grayish brown ash.

"The critter is back in the dungeons of hell where he belongs," Father Devon proudly announced.

"These unclean spirits cannot remain in a dead host," added Yacine. "They are too powerful for the birds. So they must return to the Pit."

"Does anyone know how this *Nyambii* got out in the first place?"

Yacine admitted, "This is a mystery, my friend, something that God has not completely revealed. But many believe they come through the gateway of the underworld call *Hekla*. It is the ancient volcano south of Iceland. Many holy men have seen the evil around this place."

"Monk Benedeit of Circa called it the *Prison of Judas*, and with due cause," added Father Devann. "But tonight, we have returned a great escapee back to the dungeons to serve his time. Amen?"

I stepped over to Father Devann to shake his hand. "I want to thank you for all that you've done for me and my wife. God has given you a special gift."

"God has shown favor on you, my lad. First, to have a friend like Yacine. Not to mention the hand of heaven that allowed our plane to land; it being the last flight to land before the storm. It didn't have to ... have to...."

He suddenly paused, then stumbled, then crashed to the floor.

Yacine immediately moved in to check his pulse.

"You must help me," he pleaded.

"Whh-What's wrong with him?"

"We must move him to the bed! Quickly!"

The task was easier said than done. With his large, hulking frame pasted flatly on the floor, we had to drag him, inch by grueling inch, to the bed. Once there, Yacine, still weakened by months of fasting, could only watch as I hoisted the human slab of concrete onto the mattress. Panic-stricken, and driven by an unspoken urgency, Yacine pulled and nudged and pressed Father Devann into place. Then, without warning, he shackled him to the bed.

"Have you lost your mind?" I bellowed.

Yacine glanced at his watch, a stiff expression on his face. "Downstairs, I said we must trust each other. I'm asking you to trust me now."

I pointed to Father Devann, stretched awkwardly, breathing heavily, with traces of saliva dripping from the corner of his mouth. "Are you responsible for this?"

Yacine nodded. "It is a mild sedative. It will only last for ten minutes, maybe less."

"And then what?"

"And then we must try to help him," he responded.

I shook my head with confusion. "We drugged this great man of God and put him in shackles. Is that how we help him?"

For a long while, Yacine stood at the foot of the bed, staring down at Father Devann. "He is a good man. He has helped a lot of people."

"So why do this to him?" I asked.

Yacine walked over to the sacred tray. Next to it was his leather satchel. He reached inside to remove a single white sheet, then handed it to me. It contained a drawing of Father Devann, standing in a church garden, his face, illuminated by the morning light. His whole body was covered with dark blotches, some with two, three, and in the case of the larger spots, six eyes.

"What are these spots?" I demanded.

"Demons," he sadly reported. "They are inside of him."

"I don't understand. How could that be?"

Yacine explained that Father Devann had been involved in over three hundred and fifty exorcisms. He was a man of great compassion and empathy for those helpless, possessed victims that had fallen under the shadow of evil. Over time, this empathy had worked to his own personal destruction.

"In the early years, when he was too young to know how to expel the demons, he would taunt them to come into him;

anything that would rescue the hopeless victims that cried out to him for help. This desperation started with his younger sister who dabbled with the *Galukoji* and *Ouija* Board. The things he did were not authorized. But God allowed it."

"And so he kept doing it?"

"God has not sown the fabric of life with simple threads, my friend. Even for the righteous, decisions are most complicated. If a door opens that leads away from pain and suffering, man will surely take it. You can testify to this in your own home, can you not?"

Thinking of all of the dead end roads I had traveled in search of an answer, hoping and praying that relief was just over the distant hill, I could've testified in every courtroom throughout the universe.

I finally nodded in agreement.

Yacine studied the old Franciscan's rugged face. "Father was a strong man of God, gifted in the Spirit. He had the power to control these demons. But as he has gotten older, they have begun to control him."

"There has to be someone in the ranks of the Catholic Church that can help him," I insisted.

"No one knows of his condition, except me," he explained. "And if I spoke of this great man in such a derogatory manner, who would believe me? To this day, he has been able to hide his pain. Not even His Holiness, a very dear friend in the Spirit, has the slightest inclination."

"I studied the drawing in its gruesome details. "Yacine, are you sure about this?"

"I caught him in the act, my friend."

"The act of what?"

Yacine hesitated, dreading the answer he would have to give. "Child molestation. He was trying to get the little boy's pants down."

My heart stopped beating.

Yacine continued, "That is not the Father Devann I know. Besides the changes in his personality and heavy drinking behind closed doors, the demons are perverting him. They are flooding him with evil thoughts and seducing his will. That is why I had to go to Africa. That is why I desperately needed God to tell me what to do."

"What will you do?" I pressed.

He replied in a somber tone. "It is not what I will do. It is what you will do. You will perform the service. You will set him free."

My heart stopped again. I could hear Dr. Bingham's dire warning: *If anybody decides to step off into that arena, they'd better be ordained by no less than God Almighty.*

"Are you seriously out of your mind?!!! I don't know anything about this stuff; all of these metals and gold crystals and holy towels. This is way over my head."

"It is not about what you know, my friend. It is about who you are."

"Now wait just a minute," I insisted. "What about you? You're like his protégé. You've studied under this man for years?"

"But it is you who has the mark," he reminded me.

Suffering is the highest order of service to God. Again, Dr. Bingham's words clamored in my mind.

"Don't you see," pleaded Yacine. "It was not by chance that we met at seminary. It was not by chance that you have been stabbed over and over by the great dagger of tribulations. It has all been designed for a time such as this."

Father Devann flipped his head to one side, then mumbled some garbled Latin phrase.

Yacine cringed at his growing consciousness. "Time is running out, my friend. You must decide."

"I … I don't know, man. I don't know."

"Think about it this way," he reasoned. "If your Kathy went over a cliff and a man reached down to catch her before she hit the rocks, would you try to save that man should he also slip?"

"Yes, yes I would." I responded without hesitation.

Slowly, he stretched out his trembling pawns toward the old legendary warrior. "This is that man."

I stared at Yacine with a broken spirit and surrendered heart. "What is it you want me to do?"

Chapter Nine

*I*t was 2:22am when Yacine helped me slip into the plain black surplice he had smuggled in beneath the holy towels.

"I do not know whether this garment is an instrument of tradition or whether it possesses special powers," he said. "I do know in what we face this night, we cannot take any chances."

He passed a yellow tablet to me with handwritten instructions. Before I could read the first line, however, Father Devann awakened. Observing the shackles on his hands and feet, he let out a wicked roar. The scream was ten times louder than anything Kathy had managed, and for me, slaughtered any lingering doubts about the evil he harbored inside.

Yacine handed me a bottle of holy water, different from all the rest. Its coloring was dark red like the ritual wine, thickened with some kind of oil. When I dashed a handful of droplets onto Father Devann's sweaty forehead, thirty, forty, maybe even fifty shrill voices, cried out in unison.

I began reading from the yellow tablet. "Ahhh-Almighty Ga-Ga-God, we revisit your presence, asking you to have mercy upon our feeble souls. Grant your servants favor against these Unclean Spirits! Give us your power, your wisdom and your knowledge to conquer these fiery agents of hell so that this enslaved servant will be released from their cruel possession, never again to be hurt by the bite of the ancient serpent. I beg thee in the name of the Father, Son and Holy Spirit."

Nervously following the instructions on the tablet, I pressed my St. Benedict medal against his forehead. He roared with savage resistance, expulsing a flood of white and green foam from his mouth. He pulled so hard on the shackles, the bed railing started to bend. That's when the ceiling caved in.

A hurricane is a turbulent tropical swell with a hodgepodge of fierce thunderstorms and powerful currents. Though the worst of the storm was over, a pocket of high-pressured winds and torrential rain drenched the little wood frame house and tore a gaping hole in the roof. Streams of dirty water cascaded into the room, soaking the bed and floor. A watery hole, just over my head, saturated the tablet and turned the lines of blue ink into an unreadable blue mush.

Father Devann belched out a scornful snicker, the blood-curling hiss of a thousand rattlesnakes. "You stupid bastards! Did you think you could toy with me?"

The bed railing bent a few inches more.

Wild-eyed and panic-stricken, Yacine rushed over to me with a white Bible that displayed an ancient symbol of the cross. "Read from it! Quickly!"

Using my bulky frame to shield the splattering clumps of sheetrock, I opened a page at random. "Two other men, both criminals, were also led out with him to be executed. When they came to the place call the Skull, there they crucified him, along with the criminals, one on his right, and the other on his left."

Father Devann unleashed another terrifying howl. "Bloody low class thieves, they were, Yacine. Like your mother and father back in Africa. That's why they had to be punished. That's why they had to die."

Yacine froze in silence, his eyes, bulging with shock.

"What is he talking about?" I asked.

"Stay focused, my friend. Or we will lose this battle."

We were already losing the battle to the hurricane and to Father Devann. It didn't take our cosmic connection to realize it was just a matter of time before the bed railing broke, and a three hundred pound, wild-eyed giant, filled with angry demons, consumed us both.

In the Bible, the disciples returned to Jesus in private with sad faces and defeated spirits. They asked, "Why weren't we able to cast the demon out of the boy?"

And he said, "It is because of your lack of faith."

We were no match for supernatural spirits, feeding on evil. And then it dawned on me. We weren't supposed to be. We were using ancient Bibles and holy towels and sacred metals to do our bidding. Our faith rested in the sacred relics, not in the power of Almighty God.

Christians around the world had been taught that faith was the substance of things hoped for, the evidence of things not seen. But now I realized that this was only half the story, an incomplete truth. Faith was an instrument of sequence, fortified through witnessing God's miracles over the passage of time. That's what my second chance was all about. God had turned on the faucet of suffering and floated me up onto a high mountain so I could observe his mastery, so I could stick my hands into his wounds like the Apostle Thomas, feel his power and watch him transform a hopeless and disastrous past into a glorious future.

The faith I longed for could not be attained by simply going to seminary or reading my Bible or crying out to heaven with dreary eyes. I needed to see God in action. With Kathy back from the abyss, I had seen enough. Now I needed to believe.

I did believe. We couldn't overcome evil ... but God could.

A portion of the ceiling beam crashed to the floor, wedging a small crack in the brown linoleum squares. Despite the ashy sheet rock and dirty water flowing through the crack, I could still see the ten flickering candles and hear the feeble voices of my prayer warriors. Buffalos and bird choirs were flying up to heaven. Somewhere in the cosmos, the sun stood still.

I grabbed the gold-plated cross that had hung over my fireplace and the red leather *Rituale Romanum* from which Father Devann had recited. I slammed the cross against the old Franciscan's chest and began to read. "Oh, Mighty God, how often your divine humility has triumphed; casting out the pride of our enemy..."

Father Devann screamed and threatened and sobbed.

I kept reading louder and louder, each word, energizing my inner man with conviction. "Deign to care for, bless, and sanctify those being inflamed by passion and weakness, any sickness, deceits of the foe and suspicious resentments felt by them..."

For a split second, I glanced up at Yacine. In his face spawn a rising confidence. We both knew the tide had changed. That was the moment for which we had hoped. That was also the moment the back wall came crashing down.

The storm had blown a huge wooden telephone post through the window. Its embedded transformers still crackled with live electric wires. The sparks steamed and exploded in the puddles of water on the floor, painting the room with an eerie cerulean halo.

The howling wind, murky water and sparkling wires cried out for me to stop. But I couldn't stop. The demon pot had come to a boil. It was time to tip it over and pour the contents back to hell.

I continued to read, "Oh God; release thy faithful servant from the grasp of the Evil One. Show your awesome power in this hour, this minute, this second. I implore you, Oh God, cast out these demons in the name of the Father, Son and Holy Spirit!"

There was a long silence, not just in the room or the house, but in the universe, itself. Time stopped and took a deep breath, allowing the wheel of providence to cleanse itself of evil, before it rolled on. Father Devann trembled and convulsed. And then, slowly, with gurgled screams of protest, the demons took flight. One by one the faint shadows of black flowed out of the bowels of the old Franciscan warrior. God's power, not mine, was cramming all of his past mistakes into a giant trunk, sealing it up with golden locks. Like me, like so many others who had made bad decisions on the treacherous highways of life, Father Devann was getting a second chance.

I peered out through the soggy bombs of sheetrock, the swirling wind and rain. I was eager to pass on the precarious news of victory, allow our cosmic connection to taste the impending sweetness of ritual wine. It was then I spotted Yacine, standing next to the gaping hole in the wall. His eyes were closed. His arms were stretched out toward heaven.

He had removed his gold-plated boots, silver bracelet, St Benedict necklace and purple stole. He was naked to the dark shadows that flowed into him.

"Yacine! No! Put your gear back on!" I shouted.

He didn't hear me. He was oblivious to the wind and rain and my muffled voice. He was too busy carrying out his part in the transfer of evil. The more the shadows filled him, the less connected to this world he seemed to be.

I wanted so desperately to ask him why the demons couldn't go straight to hell. Was there some unwritten law outside the sixty-six books of the Bible that Jesus had followed when he sent the demons into the hogs on the cliff? Was Father Devann obligated to use the sacrificial turtle doves? I knew he knew. He had devoted his life to knowing. But I never got the chance to ask.

The instant the last demon flowed into him, Yacine opened his eyes. With one last nod of his head, one last cosmic gesture of reassurance, he slammed his foot on the electric cable.

As the smell of burning hair and flesh overpowered the room, I could feel his mark clawing in on me like sharpened blades of revelation. It was the mark of ... sacrifice.

I could hear his words: *Don't you see? It was not by chance that we met at seminary. It was not by chance that you have been stabbed over and over by the great dagger of tribulations. It has all been designed for a time such as this.*

And then, all the lights went out.

Leander Jackie Grogan

Chapter Ten

"I know the plans I have for you, declares the Lord, plans to prosper you and not to harm you, plans to give you hope and a future...."

Jeremiah the Prophet

Six months later, Kathy and I sat on the terrace of an exclusive seafood restaurant in the Houston Galleria Mall. A trio of Christmas carolers, dressed in bright red and green uniforms, rounded each table with gifts, greetings and songs. Though their festive rendition of *Silvers Bells* and *Old Christmas Tree* was thoroughly entertaining, we were happy to see them move on. We had just left the doctor's office and were eager to review the pictures of the ultrasound.

"Okay, so what's your guess?" Brandishing a delightful smile and inquisitive glow, Kathy challenged me.

"Well, we know it's twins." I hedged, trying to keep a straight face.

She slung her silky black hair to the side. "Daahh! We know that, you idiot father-to-be. But is it two boys, two girls, what?"

At that moment my cell phone rang, rescuing me from giving her an answer.

"Yes. Yes. No, I understand ... No, I don't think that would make a difference ... Sure I'll let you know if anything changes." I hung up the phone.

"Who was it?" she asked.

"The search committee ... again."

"That Foundry Church with the large congregation?"

"Yes," I confirmed. "They wanted to know if they increased the salary and gave us housing, would I take the job. Seems their perfect fit didn't work out."

"Did you tell them we didn't care to live behind the church in one of those little cramped up, wood frame storage boxes? We've had our share of that already."

"I just told them the truth. I've started my own church and my *little* flock needs me more than their *big* flock."

A few months after the storm, Mr. Floyd, the retired oilman, died. In his will, he left some land and half a million dollars in oil and gas annuities to start a church. The only stipulation was that Reverend Rodney Coleman be the Pastor for five years. After that he didn't care. He was sure that by then, the Rapture would come and take everyone away.

"Speaking of houses. The real estate lady called. She has another house she wants you to see."

Kathy frowned. "Why, Rodney? We've already found

two we like. They're in good neighborhoods and close to the mall. Why does she keep adding to the list?"

"She told me you'd really like this one. It has sort of a country feel with a white picket fence."

"Okay, I'll look," she acquiesced. "But I'm letting her know. We're closing on something in the next thirty days."

I recognized her impatience. We had been living with Patrice for five months. Although there was plenty of room in the mini-mansion her new son-in-law, Johnnie D, had bought her, it was time for us to move on.

"Looks like this new year is going to be a blur," I predicted. "Are you sure you're up for all of this?"

"You mean restarting the catering business?"

"And going back to school, all at the same time."

"It's just a couple of night classes, Rodney. I'll be fine," she insisted. "If Aunt Bessie Mae is looking down from heaven, I know this will make her proud."

"Not as proud as me ... me and the twins."

She took my hand and gently rubbed it across her pooched stomach. Then, without warning, she dropped her head and began to cry. "I'm so sorry for giving up on you; for giving up on God. It was just so hard."

"It's okay." I stroked her bony shoulders. "What happened needed to happen, for so many reasons."

I didn't have to say it. We both knew how the years of suffering had uncovered the many flaws in our spiritual life. I never asked if she had been faking it. I just knew that now, everything was real.

"Do you forgive me?" she asked.

"Of course. I'm your husband. I love you."

"You think God forgives me?" And then, before I could answer, she replied, "I know. Don't tell me. He has a big trunk with golden locks."

"And Kathy Coleman has a second chance."

"Okay, now, I'm going to give you a second chance," she said, pointing at the photos on the table. "I'm going to the ladies' room and when I get back, I want you to tell me what you think ... boys or girls."

As I watched her disappear behind the glass doors, I smiled confidently. I already knew the answer.

The day after the storm, after Father Devann left for New York, and the police investigators completed their report, I went into the freezer and pulled out the envelope Yacine had given me. Inside, I found a short letter, a blue pouch and one of Yacine's radiantly detailed sketches.

The letter read: *Your friendship has meant so much to me. I have tried to keep it pure. But I have not been honest on all accounts. My mother and father did not die from disease. They were killed smuggling diamonds out of the country. I hope you understand why I did not want to tell you. I hope you understand everything.*

The pouch is yours to keep. The price has already been paid in blood. You will tell your children of me, yes? And I will tell God of you.

When I opened the blue pouch I had found three uncut diamonds that appraised at approximately $150,000 each. It was more than enough to start over. With my small salary from the church, I was able to quit the Post Office to begin pastoring my little Bible study flock full time.

And then, there was the drawing. It showed Kathy and me, standing in front of a house with a white picket fence. We were holding the hands of our children; little tricycle-riding twins ... a boy and a girl.

Kathy had informed the doctor she didn't want to know. So I was determined to abide by her request. I had told her about the letter and the diamonds. But the drawing would just have to wait.

There was a time for everything ... *a time to be born, and a time to die; a time to plant, and a time to pluck up that which is planted; A time to kill, and a time to heal; a time to break down, and a time to build up; A time to weep, and a time to laugh; a time to mourn, and a time to dance; A time to cast away stones, and a time to gather stones together; a time to embrace, and a time to refrain from embracing ... and a time to talk about the drawing...*

I had already spent too much time on the past and its inflated glory. I didn't want my knowledge of the future to become the same kind of stumbling block. I had decided to give the past and the future back to the universe and live out our second chance in the here-and-now.

After Virgil "Tank" Brown's death, the old woman preacher from the Presbyterian Church had told us to let it go. Let all of the hurt and sorry and pain wash away in the downpour. Take our life-lessons and move on.

That's what I would do. I would remember what God had done to us and for and in front of our very eyes. I would take my life-lessons of his magnificence, grace and power ... and then, move on.

A few minutes later, watching her return to the table, the brilliant glow of creation upon her beautiful face, I prepared my clueless expression, which, for an old dumb buffalo, was not that hard to do. What were we going to have ... two boys, two girls? Uuhmmm........?

We'd just have to wait and see.

###The End ###

Appreciation

Thank you for your encouragement and support.

Please email me with your comments:

grogan007@live.com

Twitter: @blackchurchblue

Also, and this is a big one, if you enjoyed the book, please, please take a few minutes to leave a review. A paragraph, a line, a thumb print to help new readers find their way ... I will be forever grateful.

BOOKS BY LEANDER JACKIE GROGAN

Orange FingerTips

Exorcism At Midnight

Baby, Put That Gun Down

Layoff Skullduggery: The Official Humor Guide

King Juba's Chest

The Blood Tears Of Jesus

Black Church Blues

The Bible Gobbled Up My Big Sister [Not yet released

What's Wrong With Your Small Business Team?

Demon possession is a never-ending topic of discussion that extends beyond faith, denomination, and creed.   Even with Jesus performing exorcisms in the Bible, the debate rages on as to whether demon possession continues in our modern day society.

The interest was heightened even more when the late Pope John Paul II confirmed that he had been involved in three exorcisms. Before he died, he was trying to get the official office of exorcists restored to the priesthood.

In November of 2010, over a 100 Catholic bishops and priests gathered in Baltimore for a two-day conference on exorcism, organized by a bishop who said he wanted U.S. dioceses to be prepared. The purpose of the conference was to educate the clergy members of the scriptural basis for the need for exorcism, and to teach them about how the ritual should be performed.

Bishop Thomas Paprocki of Springfield, Ill., the chairman of the bishops' Committee on Canonical Affairs and Church Governance, admitted the need for exorcisms is rare. However, it does occasionally arise.

There is a gray area of subjective analysis that must occur in order to distinguish demon possession from ordinary psychological disorders such as Tourette syndrome and schizophrenia. Both can produce the types of effects seen in "possessed" people.

People with epilepsy can suddenly go into convulsions when having a seizure; Tourette syndrome causes involuntary movements and vocal outbursts; schizophrenia involves auditory and visual hallucinations, paranoia, delusions and sometimes violent behavior. Psychological issues like low self-esteem and narcissism can cause a person to act out of character in order to gain attention. In a case where the subject is in fact suffering from mental illness, the Church is doing harm by labeling the person possessed.

When someone reports a possible case of possession to the Church, an investigation begins. Back in the 70's and 80's, Father Benedict Groeschel, a Franciscan priest who holds a Ph.D. in psychology from Columbia University, was the man the Archdiocese of New York called on to investigate such cases.

"When cases were referred to me I usually sought the help of a laywoman in the archdiocese who possessed a gift for discerning spirits," explained Father Groeschel. "As it turned out, none the people I brought to her were victims of possession. None of them were in need of formal exorcism."

A typical investigation is essentially a process of elimination: Does the subject exhibit the telltale signs of demonic possession:

• Speaking or understanding languages which the person has never learned (different from "speaking in tongues," which is considered a sign of religious ecstasy, not possession)

• Knowing (and revealing) things the person has no earthly way of knowing

• Physical strength beyond the person's natural physical makeup

• A violent aversion to God, the Virgin Mary, the cross and other images of Catholic faith

If not, what type of professional intervention is necessary to get the individual back on the road to a safe and healthy existence. If so, what form of spiritual intervention, including an exorcism, is appropriate for this situation.

While Father Groeschel's investigations did not produce valid cases of demon possession, the results were totally different for Jesuit Priest Malachi Martin, a self-proclaimed exorcist and controversial figure in the Catholic world. Martin found many people in need of an exorcism. In his book, *Hostage to the Devil*, Martin revealed what he considers to be the typical stages of an exorcism (Cuneo 19-20), once a collaborative decision of demonic possession had been made:

1. Pretense - The demon is hiding its true identity.

2. Breakpoint - The demon reveals itself.

3. Clash - The exorcist and the demon fight for the soul of the possessed.

4. Expulsion - If the exorcist wins the battle, the demon leaves the body of the possessed.

About The Exorcism

There are official rules. The following rules pertain to the instruction of the Exorcist as indicated in the Old Rite - Rules of the Roman Ritual of Exorcism.

(RULE 1) The priest who with the particular and explicit permission of his Bishop is about to exorcise those tormented by Evil Spirit, must have the necessary piety, prudence and personal integrity. He should perform this most heroic work humbly and courageously, not relying on his own strength, but on the power of God; and he must have no greed for material benefit. Besides, he should be of mature age and be respected as a virtuous person.

(RULE 5) Let the exorcist note for himself the tricks and deceits which evil spirits use in order to lead him astray. For they are accustomed to answering falsely. They manifest themselves only under pressure--in the hope that the exorcist will get tired and desist from pressuring them. Or they make it appear that the subject of Exorcism is not possessed at all.

(RULE 6) Sometimes, Evil Spirit betrays its presence, and then goes into hiding. It appears to have left the body of the possessed free from all molestation, so that the possessed thinks he is completely rid of it. But the exorcist should not, for all that, desist until he sees the signs of liberation.

(RULE 10) The Exorcist must remember, therefore, that Our Lord said there is a species of Evil Spirit which cannot be expelled except by prayer and fasting. Let him make sure that he and others follow the example of the Holy Fathers and make use of these two principal means of obtaining divine help and of repelling Evil Spirit.

(RULE 20) During Exorcism, the exorcist should use the words of the Bible rather than his own or somebody else's. Also, he should command Evil Spirit to state whether it is kept within the possessed because of some magical spell or sorcerer's symbol or some occult documents. For the exorcism to succeed, the possessed must surrender them. If he has swallowed something like that, he will vomit it up. If it is outside his body in some place or other, Evil Spirit must tell the exorcist where it is. When the exorcist finds it, he must burn it.

In order for Satan to be driven out of the possessed, the exorcist must be humble. He must rely on God and only God for his answers and direction. Sometimes God forces the demon inside the possessed to reveal truths.

There are many other rules that govern the exorcism service. The point is training and preparation are key.

Examples of Modern Day Exorcisms

Unfortunately, botched exorcisms receive more publicity than those deemed successful. By nature, exorcisms directed by God's hand should be secret and unsensational. Thus, as we examine the exorcisms about which we know, we find a skewed result mired in disaster.

Here are a few:

Attempted Exorcism Ends in Phoenix Man's Death

PHOENIX - Officers responding to a report of an exorcism on a young girl found her grandfather choking her and used stun guns to subdue the man, who later died, authorities said Sunday.

The 3-year-old girl and her mother, who was also in the room during the struggle between 49-year-old Ronald Marquez and officers, were hospitalized, police said. Their condition was unavailable. The relative who called police said an exorcism had also been attempted Thursday. "The purpose was to release demons from this very young child," said Sgt. Joel Tranter.

Officers arrived at the house Saturday and entered when they heard screaming coming from a bedroom, Tranter said. Naked woman seen chanting A bed had been pushed up against the door; the officers pushed it open a few inches and saw Marquez choking his bloodied granddaughter, who was crying in pain and gasping, Tranter said. A bloody, naked 19-year-old woman who police later determined to be Marquez's daughter and the girl's mother was in the room, chanting "something that was religious in nature," Tranter said.

The officers forced open the door enough for one to enter, leading to a struggle in which an officer used a stun gun on Marquez, Tranter said. Mother may be charged After the initial stun had no visible effect, another officer squeezed into the room and stunned him. The girl was freed and passed through the door to the relative. Marquez was placed in handcuffs after a struggle with officers and initially appeared normal, but then stopped breathing, Tranter said. He could not be revived and was pronounced dead at a hospital.

Tranter declined to identify Marquez's daughter and granddaughter but said they lived in the house with Marquez. The mother was not arrested, but police will consider criminal charges, Tranter said. There was no phone listing at Ronald Marquez's address. When reading this article, you will find many things that seem bizarre. I would like to hear your comments. I will give you a hint on one. How many times did they have to stun the man... and why did he seem normal after so many stuns?

Milwaukee Boy Dies During Exorcism

MILWAUKEE - An autistic 8-year-old boy died while wrapped in sheets during a prayer service held to exorcise the evil spirits that church members blamed for his condition.

The minister who performed the service was arrested in connection with the death, which occurred Friday night at a church in a run-down strip mall.

The mother had been taking her son to Faith Temple Church of the Apostolic Faith three times a week for the last three weeks in hopes of curing his autism, said Bishop David Hemphill Sr.

It was after more than an hour of prayer that a parishioner noticed the boy was no longer moving and called emergency workers, Hemphill said. The boy's grandmother said force was used, an allegation disputed by church members.

"We were asking God to take this spirit that was tormenting this little boy to death," Hemphill said. "We were praying that hard, but not to kill."

Hemphill identified the boy as Torrance Cantrell and the man arrested as Ray Hemphill, his brother and another minister who led Friday's service. David Hemphill said he has not talked to his brother or the boy's mother, Patricia Cooper, since Friday night. Cooper could not be reached for comment.

Church members had wrapped the boy in sheets to keep him from scratching himself and others, but he was allowed to sit "any way that he feels comfortable," Hemphill said.

The boy's grandmother said the boy had been restrained.

"They held the boy down, they held him down until ... he went to a smothery grave," Mary Luckett told Milwaukee television station WTMJ.

The Milwaukee Journal Sentinel reported that David Hemhill's wife, Pamela Hemphill, said that Torrance's mother held the boy's feet and two other women held the boy's hands during the prayer session.

Cooper, the boy's mother, started coming to the church about three months ago after she met a parishioner at a doctor's office, Hemphill said. Cooper told the parishioner about her son's autism, and the church member invited her to a Sunday service. She joined the next week.

<hr />

Young Mother Drowns in Maori Exorcism
By Paul Chapman in Wellington

NEW ZEALAND - A young mother drowned after having water continually poured down her throat in a Maori exorcism, a court in New Zealand has been told.

Janet Moses, 22, was held down on the floor of a house during the three-day long ceremony to lift a traditional curse, or makutu, prosecutors say.

Six men and three women, whose names have been suppressed by the court, pleaded not guilty to the manslaughter of Ms Moses in Wellington.

One of the women and a seventh man are also charged with ill-treating a 14-year-old girl, after her eyes were allegedly gouged when the evil spirit was thought to have moved on to her.

Kate Feltham, prosecuting, told the High Court that Ms Moses, a mother-of-two, drowned during a "cleansing ceremony" at a house in Wainuiomata, near Wellington, in October 2007.

"Janet was held down on the floor while her eyelids were forced open. Water was poured down her face and in her eyes in an attempt to get rid of the makutu," Ms Feltham said. "Several people also leant over Janet, put their mouths over her eyeballs, and tried to suck at her eyes in an attempt, again, to remove the curse."

The Exorcism of Anneliese Michel

Besides the exorcisms that Jesus performed in the Bible, this is probably the most famous one of all. Three motion pictures, *The Exorcism of Emily Rose, Requiem, and the Asylum film Anneliese* were based on this spectacular event.

Born in 1952, Anneliese Michel was a German Catholic woman who was said to be possessed by demons and subsequently underwent an exorcism. The case has been labelled as a misidentification of mental illness, negligence, abuse, and religious hysteria. But no one can say for sure.

In 1969, seventeen-year-old Anneliese began a journey from which she would not return. One day, without any reasonable explanation, Anneliese's body began to shake. At a nearby clinic, physicians diagnosed her as having a grand mal epileptic seizure for which she was treated.

Perhaps, it was the demon imps that appeared to her as faces on the wall whenever she tried to pray or the evil voices that whispered in her ear. But, Anneliese felt the doctors were wrong.

Anneliese pleaded to her psychiatrist, telling him the voices were trying to control her. He responded by prescribing anti-psychotic drugs.

Finally, Anneliese and her parents sought spiritual help. They eventually found Father Ernst Alt who sought permission from the church to perform the exorcism. The church rejected his request, however, and told the family to pray and increase their faith in God.

Anneliese continued to decline. She began eating insects and attacking family members. She seldom bathed and used sharp objects to pierce her skin. She became nothing more than a dehydrated skeleton.

Finally, the church authorized a Rituale Romanum exorcism. Multiple priest had to hold her down, and eventually, restrain her in heavy chains. This *temporarily* allowed her to live a normal life and return to school in Aschefenburg. But without warning, the symptoms came back, only worse this time. Anneliese began experiencing paralysis of her entire body and total black outs.

Father Alt, along with the main exorcist, Father Arnold Renz, and the friends and family, resumed the exorcism ritual. It continued for months, nonstop, day and night. But nothing they did seemed to help.

By the summer of '76, suffering from pneumonia and fever, Anneliese was near death. Sorrowfully, she begged for absolution and then passed away.

In a twist of events, the priests and family were charged with negligent homicide in Anneliese's death. At the trial, doctors testify to the girl's insanity as supported by a series of recorded tapes that were made during the various sessions. Yet, they could not explain why their years of medication had not worked.

During the case Anneliese's body was exhumed and tapes were played to the court of the exorcisms over the eleven months leading to her death. In the end, the state asked that no involved parties be jailed; instead the recommended sentence for the priests was a fine. The prosecution asked the parents be recused from punishment as they had "suffered enough".

You may go here to hear actual audio recordings of the exorcism sessions.

WARNING: These recordings are very disturbing and my not be suited for your listening tolerance.

http://diabolicalconfusions.wordpress.com/2011/03/14/the-entire-case-history-of-anneliese-michel-the-real-emily-rose-warning-shocking-content/

Biblical References on Demon Possession

In closing, the Bible is our ultimate source of truth for understanding the supernatural world and demon possession in particular. Please take time to research, study and meditate on these scriptures. Remember, we will never know every aspect to this phenomenon. We continue to learn day by day.

For now we see through a glass, darkly; but then face to face: now I know in part; but then shall I know even as also I am known....

Symptoms of demonic influence and possession

Matthew 9:32-33; 12:22; 17:18; Mark 5:1-20; 7:26-30; Luke 4:33-36; Luke 22:3; Acts 16:16-18; Acts 16:16-18.

Physical or emotional distinctions

Corinthians 2:10-1; 2 Corinthians 11:3-4, 13-15; 1 Timothy 4:1-5; 1 John 4:1-3.

Believers influenced by the devil

Matthew 16:23; 2 Corinthians 1:22; 5:5; 1 Corinthians 6:19.

Idol worship of demons

Leviticus 17:7; Deuteronomy 32:17; Psalm 106:37.

www.ingramcontent.com/pod-product-compliance
Lightning Source LLC
Chambersburg PA
CBHW020504100426
42813CB00030B/3119/J